A History of
THE FIRST PRESBYTERIAN CHURCH BELFAST
⊰⊹⊱ 1644~1983 ⊰⊹⊱

COMPILED BY TOM MOORE, JOINT HON. SECRETARY

Front cover: Print of Meeting-house erected in 1783.
(from an engraving by J. Thomson)

Published by The First Presbyterian Church,
Rosemary Street, Belfast 1983

ISBN   0   9502645   1   2

Printed by Priory Press, Holywood, Co. Down.

CONTENTS

Page

Chapter 1.   Introduction: Reformation in England, Scotland and
             Ireland; Presbyterian settlement in Ulster and Belfast.   2

Chapter 2.   Congregational Property: Grounds; Church; Pews;
             Heating; Lighting; Memorials; Bomb Damage; Central
             Hall; Air Raids; Rebuilding Hall; Manses.   27

Chapter 3.   Congregational Administration: Session; General
             Committee; Music Committee; Sub-committees;
             Other Organisations; Constituency and Membership;
             Finance.   54

Chapter 4.   Church Services: Frequency; Order of Service;
             Communion Services; Broadcast Services.   84

Chapter 5.   Church Music: Early Choir; Installation of Organs;
             Selection of Music.   92

Chapter 6.   Sunday School and Library: Foundation and
             Operation.   100

Chapter 7.   The Church and Schools: Belfast Academy; Academi-
             cal Institution; Fountain Street Schools; Riddel
             Memorial School.   103

Chapter 8.   The Church in the Community: Charity Sermons;
             Special Collections; City Authorities; America and
             Europe; Political Attitudes.   112

Chapter 9.   The Theological Stance of the Congregation: The
             Necessary Representation; Non-Subscription and
             Unitarianism; Secularism and Religious Bigotry.   125

Appendices: Congregational Records; Ministers; Singing Clerks
             and Organists; Church Officers; Trustees; Bequests;
             The Changing value of the Pound; Lists of Members.   136

FOREWORD

There have been two previous histories of the First Presbyterian Congregation of Belfast. Both Alexander Gordon's of 100 years ago and R.W. Wilde's of 1944 were written by ministers and might be said to contain as much polemic as history. This history is by a layman, Mr. Tom Moore, who has most carefully gone through the available records to present the First Congregation in its living continuity. There is no blind ancestor-worship within its pages; and that is as it should be for Ulster has been too often cursed by romanticised and parochial views of the past which bedevil our understanding of the present day.

Here in over three hundred years of ongoing city life will be found moments of great involvement and moments of near deafness to the needs around, times of strength and times of weakness, occasions of bitter controversy and occasions of glorious Christian good-will, periods of Victorian self-satisfaction and events in which the congregation has been driven to the bed-rock of its faith to find the strength to go on. All these not only make this a most valuable document — historically, sociologically and religiously — but are a pointer to the type of honesty in looking to the past which this new age needs. I am proud to feel that Mr. Moore has produced this book during my time as the minister of the First Congregation, and congratulate him on a fine task well done.

Mr. Moore set out to prepare this book for the 200th Anniversary of our present meeting-house in Rosemary Street. Until 1897 the First, Second and Third Presbyterian Congregations of Belfast were all situated in Rosemary Street. Now only the First remains on its historic site. As the story unfolds it will no doubt be appreciated that the congregation has moved a long way in its thought since Halliday first expressed his doubts about subscribing to the Westminster Confession of Faith. On the other hand, I believe the unfolding reveals the congregation's long held loyalty to, and insistence upon, the value of truth in religion. And surely, God is the God of Truth or nothing but an idol of the mind, incapable of guidance and unworthy of a thoughtful man's faith and worship. It is the story of man's ongoing search for truth that pervades this book through and through.

D.G. Banham

PREFACE

The original objective of this work was to assemble a summarised account of the congregation and its property for the convenience of future office-bearers as experience had shown that busy office-bearers do not have time to search through the increasingly voluminous records for information that might be valuable to current committees. This involved collecting numerous pieces of information and attempting to group them into categories of related items. A narrative account of various aspects was then prepared and at that stage it was decided that much of the material would be of interest to a wider public and that it should be published. The objective of the work was then extended to an attempt to place the congregation in its historical, political and religious context for the general reader who is interested in its origin and characteristics, and also to provide a basic groundwork for future researchers who may wish to probe more deeply into particular aspects of the subject.

The original documents have been quoted freely but, to avoid tedium, it was often necessary to paraphrase them. In doing so the original language and style have been retained as far as possible in order to preserve the atmosphere of the times. A considerable degree of repetition of the same incident in different contexts was inevitable in the initial stages of the work and this has not been entirely edited out as it is thought that the convenience of such repetition in different sections outweighs any slight irritation it may engender.

I am grateful to the Ulster Historical Foundation, Messrs. Thames & Hudson Ltd., and others who allowed me to quote from their publications.

I am also grateful to Mr. Ralph Trueick who prepared the material for chaper 5 on church music; to the Rev. D.G.C. Banham who read through successive drafts and gave much helpful advice and assistance and to Messrs. Jim Geery and Wm. McCay who assisted with the final editing. I am particularly indebted to Mrs. Isabel McMurray who typed the drafts and the final copy. Finally I am much indebted to the church committee for their decision to publish and hope that their expectation of a wider interest in it will be realised.

Tom Moore

June 1983.

CHAPTER 1

INTRODUCTION

This account of the First Presbyterian Church, Rosemary Street, Belfast, has been prepared to celebrate the bicentenary of the present church building in 1983. The material for it is taken mainly from the congregation's own records, minutes, annual reports, calendars etc; but as the earliest records held go back only to 1760 it has been necessary to add information about the establishment of presbyterianism and the origins of the Belfast congregation from other sources. It is hoped that this account will be valuable not only to those responsible for the care and preservation of this, the oldest ecclesiastical building in Belfast, but also to those interested in the development of religious institutions and the light which they shed on men's thoughts and ideas.

Among the motives underlying the foundation of religious institutions two appear to be widespread and dominant. First is man's intuitive feeling that the universe with all its ordered content must have been devised by some intelligent superhuman power and for some particular purpose. Against this intuitive background certain events and specific individual lives are seen as revealing something of that purpose and, hence, of the nature of the creative power itself. And second, is man's apprehension of an afterlife and what it may hold in store for him after his brief sojourn on this earth. To be effective in catering for these motives a church must have an explanation for existence which men can believe — in which they can have a justifiable faith in the knowledge of the age. Thus a church tends to build up a body of beliefs or temporal dogma on this timeless intuitive foundation and to hand down these dogma to succeeding generations.

But this is where the trouble starts; while one generation may develop for itself an acceptable and justifiable faith, succeeding generations with new knowledge about the physical universe are likely to reach different conclusions on some matters. There is thus likely to be conflict between those who wish to present their "religious truths" as eternal, fixed and final for all time and those who find them out of date and unacceptable and wish to re-state their concept of truth in harmony with current knowledge.

Typical of the former was the medieval Roman Catholic Church with its body of dogma, mysterious ritual and absolution for the repentant faithful which was all powerful in controlling the lives of men down to detailed daily conduct. Speaking of the influence of the Church of Rome in England before the reformation Lindsay Keir (1) says:

"More important even than the material wealth of the Church was its sway over the minds and consciences of men. Its sacraments mediated the Grace of God to mankind; exclusion from its fold meant after death an extremity of torment which painted wall and window displayed with dreadful impressiveness to the eyes of ignorant and illiterate worshippers. Combining as they did, control over the material wealth of this world and the treasures awaiting the faithful in the next, the clergy pervaded with their influence every aspect of medieval life."

To remain successful in maintaining this dominating influence the church had to guard against the differing opinions of questioning minds — against heresy which might confuse the faithful and weaken the church's authority. In spite of the close knit structure of the church with its heirarchy of prelates and authoritarian Pope which fostered cohesion, differences of opinion did arise from time to time over the centuries. Although these differences in religious views not infrequently coincided with, and were fuelled by, differences in economic and political attitudes as R.I. Moore (2) has pointed out, they were nevertheless based on differing ideas of religious faith and practice.

With the Renaissance, pressure for change reached explosive levels, and although again increased by political and economic factors as emphasised by Father Corbishly writing in *Living Faiths* (3), it had, as he admits, its roots in the failure of the church to match the needs of the age:

"Luther applied the match to an explosive mass; there might well have been others to produce a similar effect. In the complete social, economic, political and religious situation it seems all too probable that some major upheaval was inevitable. The lethargy which perpetually menaces all settled institutions had not spared the Church; careerism and indolence corrupted the higher levels of the clergy; the lower levels of the clergy contained too many ignorant, easy-going priests; the great religious Orders had declined from their ancient ideals of austerity and unworldliness. The involvement of the temporal interests of the Papacy with current political struggles made it inevitable that the Church's policy should be invariably suspect in the eye of the great powers now emerging into national self-consciousness."

And so the Protestant Reformation of the sixteenth century spearheaded by Luther, Zwingli and Calvin gained a secure foothold throughout Europe. Commenting on the result of the Reformation in England Lindsay Keir wrote:

"Under Henry VIII the authority of the See of Rome over the provinces of Canterbury and York was rejected. The result was not the establishment of a Church henceforth independent alike of papal and royal supremacy, but one wholly subordinated to the Crown."

The English Reformation Parliament met on 3 November 1529 and various measures were introduced which weakened papal control over affairs in England. Henry's case for the annulment of his marriage to Catherine was prepared. The Pope issued a prohibition in November 1532 against the annulment but Henry ignored the prohibition and married Anne secretly in January 1533. Thomas Cranmer was consecrated Archbishop of Canterbury by the Pope in March 1533 and he tried the King's case in May, finding for the King. Parliament then passed the Act in Restraint of Appeals which proclaimed the King supreme in both temporal and spiritual matters thus preventing an appeal to the Pope on Catherine's behalf. The King's position was further strengthened by the Act of Supremacy passed by Parliament in 1534 which accepted the King "as the only supreme head in earth of the Church of England." Although later repudiated by Mary it was re-enacted along with the Act of Uniformity in Queen Elizabeth I's reign with the modification that Elizabeth held the title "Supreme Governor" instead of "Supreme Head" at her own express wish.

These measures sealed the break with Rome but left the authoritarian structure of the church unchanged. Some of the more radical protestants looked for greater independence for the church to regulate its own affairs leading to a sharp division in the first reformed Convocation in 1563. The reformers were defeated narrowly by 59 votes to 58, resulting in the re-establishment of the Book of Common Prayer and, with some changes, the return of Cranmer's Thirty Nine Articles of Religion. Lindsay Keir identifies the years 1566-7 as witnessing a constitutional divide when the episcopate began to align itself with the Crown and become the instrument of royal authority rather than of the church's will.

However, non-conformity was still active; unauthorised religious meetings increased in number and Keir remarks:

"even more dangerous was the tendency for an informal Presbyterian organisation to introduce itself."

This tendency was, no doubt, stimulated and encouraged by the activities of John Knox in Scotland. After Grindal came to Canterbury in 1575 a privately compiled Book of Discipline provided a pattern for a non-episcopal organisation within the church. However, his successor in 1583, John Whitgift, dealt severely with this nascent presbyterian organisation within the church and other irregularities in worship, some inspired by the Brownists, the forerunners of Independency who aimed at the supremacy of individual congregations. Parliament made several bids during Elizabeth's reign to loosen episcopal authority but the Queen steadfastly prevented its interference. Keir sums up the situation at the end of her reign thus:

"Coercion seemed to have done its work. Crown, hierarchy and Convocation stood together. Parliament had effected nothing."

In Scotland, before the Union, the reformation led by John Knox took quite a different course, adopting a Calvinist theology and a presbyterian form of church government, though not without a long struggle against prelacy. The Protestant religion was formally established by an Act of the Scottish Parliament in 1560. The first Book of Discipline produced in 1561 allowed a limited form of episcopacy and the Convention of Leith in 1572 re-established the hierarchy. But in 1581 the second Book of Discipline from the hand of Andrew Melville, Knox's successor, swept away all traces of episcopacy. James VI of Scotland, though familiar with presbyterianism and interested in Calvinist theology, felt the need to control the church in support of his belief in the divine right of kings. The so-called Black Acts of 1584 supported the King's ecclesiastical authority and reaffirmed bishops, castigating the "new pretended presbyteries." But in 1592 the full presbyterian system was restored and bishops banished. The King continued to assert his divine right and authority as head of the church but the Kirk held that the King, though principal magistrate, was subject to the direction of the Kirk. James tried to get the Kirk to nominate bishops to the Scottish Parliament at the Assembly of 1600, but it refused. He later appointed bishops himself.

At the Hampton Court conference in 1604 James (by then James I of Great Britain and Ireland) favoured the High Church party, and ninety ministers in England were deprived of their livings for non-conformity. Lindsay Keir says that the King confused the Puritans of England with the theocratic presbyterians of Scotland leading to this hasty and ill-considered expulsion which gained the sympathy of the House of Commons for the Puritans and resulted in its becoming the focus of opposition to the King. James eventually succeeded in getting the Scottish General Assembly to accept an episcopal organisation in 1610, and Charles I carried the process further by prescribing in 1633 the Anglican surplice instead of the geneva gown, introducing a new set of canons in 1635 and a new Prayer Book on Anglican lines in 1637. This was too much for the Kirk; the uproar which it provoked led to the National Covenant "in defence of the King's majesty, his person and authority .... and of true religion." What was meant by "true religion" was made clear in November 1638 when the General Assembly decreed the extinction of the episcopate and the abolition of the service book and the canons. This led to armed conflict (the Bishops wars) in which the King was defeated, but he still adhered firmly to his view that ecclesiastical supremacy belonged to the Crown alone, and not the Crown in Parliament, and that the constituted authorities of the church formed the sole valid instrument for its exercise.

The opposers in the Long Parliament, known as the Root and Branch men, from their determination to extirpate episcopacy root and branch, were agreed on what they did not want but could not agree on a reformed plan of church government and ritual. Some supported a presbyterian system of church government while others contended that individual congregations should independently decide their own government and forms of worship. Consequently their effect was weakened. But the King weakened his own support by attempting to impeach the opposition leaders in 1642, causing a deep schism in Parliament and the country and leading to the first Civil War.

The reformers in the English Parliament now sought assistance from Scotland and entered into the Solemn League and Covenant with the Scots, thus reinforcing the presbyterian influence. A joint committee of both kingdoms was formed to direct affairs under Parliamentary control. Among other measures this Committee established an Assembly of Divines at Westminster in July 1643 to advise Parliament on matters affecting religion. It was this

Assembly which produced the Westminster Confession of Faith in 1648. They also produced a Directory of Public Worship in 1645 and a plan for the reorganisation of parishes on presbyterian lines.

In 1647 the Scots army, to whom Charles I had surrendered himself in 1646, having failed to force the King to accept the Solemn League and Covenant, handed him over to the English Parliament and withdrew to Scotland.

At this time the English Parliament was relatively weak and dominated by the English army of which Keir says:

"Recruited on principles which admitted no distinction between Protestants of all varieties, among whom Independents and Congregationalists predominated, it would never accept and enforced conformity whether Episcopal or Presbyterian"; and "The rank and file permeated by the influence of the Leveller party inspired by Lilburne, based all power on democratic consent."

They repudiated the House of Lords but still adhered to the idea of a parliamentary monarchy. Parliament, not approving of the army's constitutional and religious views and being both unwilling and unable to pay it, decided to disband the army which retaliated by seizing the King at Holmby House. In July 1647 the officers offered the King "heads of proposals" which included a limited monarchy, toleration for religion outside an episcopal establishment and a written constitution. Keir comments:

"The monarchism of the army officers, still further attenuated by their conviction that it was necessary to deny the King any negative voice in legislation, yielded before the republicanism of the Levelling rank and file, expressed in the non-monarchial and anti-parliamentary Agreement of the People. Charles's Engagement with the Scots, by which Presbyterianism was to have a three-years provisional establishment in England, unloosed the Second Civil War, in which the Scots were defeated, the Engagement was wrecked, and republicanism triumphed in the army. Parliament did what it could to save the King by entering upon the Treaty of Newport for concessions as to the armed forces and appointments to office which he was prepared to consider, and an establishment of Presbyterianism which he was not. But Parliament was now helpless. Pride's Purge ejected in December 1648 the Presbyterian supporters of monarchy. The Rump which remained passed an Ordinance for the King's trial by a High Court of Justice. To this illegal tribunal he refused to plead and by it he was on 27th January 1649 sentenced to death."

A Commonwealth was now declared by "the representatives of the people in Parliament . . . without either King or House of Lords". But the Rump Parliament combined the executive with the legislative and interfered with the judiciary, alienating the mass of the population and creating a situation which led to its abolition by the army in April 1653. The army now attempted to establish rule by an aristocracy of the "godly" and set up the Barebones Parliament; but in spite of good intentions it failed and was replaced by a strong executive composed of a Protector (Cromwell) and Council and a unicameral Parliament. The army maintained its neutral attitude to religion, being content to prevent any faction from gaining dominance. Cromwell himself was an Independent of surprising liberalism for the age and the attitude of the Council was typified by its Latin Secretary — John Milton.

No satisfactory relationship between the Protector and Parliament was devised and when Cromwell died in 1658 the movement for the restoration of the monarchy as a means of resolving the chaos rapidly gathered momentum. The English army of occupation in Scotland under Monk marched south to Westminster in January 1660 and forced the Long Parliament to readmit the members expelled by Pride in 1648 and eventually to dissolve itself. A convention containing a presbyterian majority was now assembled and proceeded to arrange for the restoration of the monarchy.

Charles II had issued a Declaration at Breda which, among other provisions, promised "a liberty to tender consciences, and that no man shall be disquieted or called in question for differences of opinion in matters of religion, which do not disturb the peace of the Kingdom." But the Convention Parliament failed to implement this promise and the presbyterians rejected a proposal for a unified national church containing both Anglicans and presbyterians with a limited episcopacy. And so the pendulum of opinion swung once more against the presbyterians. The Cavalier Parliament repudiated the Solemn League and Covenant and passed the Act of Uniformity in 1662 leading to the ejection of 2000 clergy who dissented from the Anglican rites and forms.

The King attempted to modify Parliament's extreme measures and uphold his Breda Declaration, but the Commons held that the promises made at Breda were a mere statement of the King's personal intention to which no effect could be given except by statute. Thus in England dissent was suppressed for many years while in Scotland the presbyterian system of church government was firmly established.

In Ireland the reformation took a different course. In the pre-reformation church in Ireland the hierarchy, appointed by mutual agreement between the Pope and Crown, was predominantly non-Irish and non-Irish speaking. They were out of touch with the poorly educated lower clergy and the mass of the people. There is little evidence of pressure from within the church in Ireland for reform in the sixteenth century but changes were imposed by the immigrant protestants from Henry VIII's time onwards. Perhaps that very circumstance inhibited any reform movement within the church. Roman Catholic bishops and priests who did not become protestants were replaced by reformers and it was the shortage of people for the Anglican priesthood that facilitated the appointment of many Scottish ministers with presbyterian leanings.

The earlier plantation of Ireland in Elizabethan times had been mainly by English settlers; but when James I thought to solve the Irish problem by increasing the rate of plantation he turned to Scotland, where emigrants could be found for whom conditions in Ireland would be less harsh than in their native country. This movement was later reinforced by the Scottish Parliament which strongly favoured the settlement of Scots in the north-east part of Ireland after the threat of the invasion of Scotland from Ireland by Strafford's army in 1639. Among those who came in the early seventeenth century was a number of presbyterian ministers who were opposed to the established episcopacy in the now Protestant Church of Ireland. As Reid (4) comments:

"The nonconformists had been consequently obliged to leave the kingdom (i.e. Scotland). Many of them fled to Ireland and they were advanced to influential situations both in the university and the church; for provided they were removed out of England and Scotland, where they so frequently opposed his arbitrary measures, James cared little for their existence and influence in this remote and turbulent country."

The Scottish settlers tended to concentrate in the north eastern counties and Scottish ministers came to Ballycarry, Antrim, Carrickfergus, Muckamore, Templepatrick and Donegore. It is generally agreed that the first presbyterially ordained minister to come over was the Rev. Edward Brice who was inducted to Ballycarry in 1613; he was followed by the Rev. Robert Cunningham who came to Holywood in 1615. These Scottish ministers were appointed to parish churches, some being episcopally ordained and others refusing such ordination. For example when Robert Blair refused episcopal ordination the liberal Bishop Echlin of Down agreed to join with other ministers in a presbyterian type of ordination at Bangor in 1623.

However when Blair and Livingston (who came to Killinchy in 1630) visited Scotland in 1630 to assist in the administration of the Lord's Supper at Kirk of Shotts they "poured fourth such invectives against Popery and Prelacy that the Bishop of Glasgow represented the matter to Leslie, Dean of Down, who laid the complaint before Bishop Echlin." (Montgomery 5) Echlin deposed them but they appealed to the Primate, Ussher, at whose request Echlin reinstated them. The Scottish prelates then appealed to Charles I through Archbishop Laud and obtained an order from the Lord Justices of Ireland to try Blair and Livingston and two other ministers for non-conformity. On their refusal to subscribe the Articles of the Church they were deposed in 1632.

Blair then took the case to the King and obtained a letter from the King to Wentworth, who had just been appointed Lord Lieutenant, ordering the restoration of the ministers, a considerable achievement in view of the King's preoccupation with attempting to establish episcopacy elsewhere. When Wentworth arrived in Ireland in 1633 Blair presented the letter but Wentworth refused to implement the King's command until Lord Castlestewart intervened on behalf of the ministers. This might have ended the matter had not John Bramhall come to Ireland with Wentworth on Archbishop Laud's recommendation. He was appointed Bishop of Derry, and Leslie had succeeded Echlin as Bishop of Down.

A convocation of clergy in Dublin in 1634 produced Articles for the Irish Church conforming with those in England and replacing the Calvinistic Articles produced by Ussher in 1615. Bramhall and Leslie now renewed their attack on the recalcitrant ministers, requiring their subscription to the new Canons. This led to the meeting in Belfast on 11 August 1636 between Leslie and Bramhall and five ministers who refused to subscribe. An account of this three-day encounter given by Reid indicates that the main objections of the presbyterians to subscribing the articles were because of the selective nature of the Scriptures on which the Prayer Book was based and to some practices, especially kneeling at communion, a topic which occupied much of the discussion. Bishop Leslie in the course of the debate made the perceptive remark that "a man may commit idolatry as well sitting as kneeling." On the whole Leslie treated his opponents with respect and an obvious measure of sympathy in marked contrast to Bramhall (who joined the meeting after it had been in progress some time). His first interjection was "My Lord of Down, in good faith, I commend your charity, but not your wisdom in suffering such a prattling jack (i.e. one of the ministers) to talk so openly against the orders of the church. My Lord it is more than you can justify yourself to the State." and later "It were more reason and more fit this fellow were whipped than reasoned with."

On the final day Leslie said: "My masters I thought to have gained you to our church and was willing to have taken more pains upon you. But now I am informed I went further in allowing public dispute than I can justify by law, so that I must not go on in that kind," Apparently Bramhall had seen the risk of public discussion and put pressure on Leslie to bring the debate to an end and deprive the ministers of their platform. The ministers were again deposed.

Belfast was apparently mainly an English settlement at this time, having developed after the rebuilding of O'Neill's castle by Sir Arthur Chichester in 1612. There is no record of any clergyman with presbyterian inclinations having officiated there before 1642. When the rebellion broke out in 1641 the English Parliament was unable to spare troops to protect the English and Scottish settlers in Ireland and was concerned with the possibility of armed support for the King by an Irish army invading Scotland. To fill this void arrangements were made with the Scottish Parliament to send an army to Ulster.

The prospects for presbyterians in Ulster changed radically with the arrival of this Scottish army under General Robert Monro at Carrickfergus in 1642. The treaty between the English and Scottish Parliaments for sending this army allocated to it the ports of Carrickfergus and Coleraine but Belfast was not mentioned. However, apparently one third of a Scots regiment was quartered in Belfast, for at the first Presbytery, consisting of ministers and elders from the Scottish regiments, which met at Carrickfergus on 10th June 1642, Mr. Baird, chaplain in Argyle's regiment, was appointed to preach in Belfast every third Sunday (Adair 6). According to Stevenson (7) these troops were withdrawn from Belfast early in 1644 when preparations were being made to send back the Scots army to assist against the King's forces in England; but when this plan was abandoned and Monro appointed Commander in Chief of both Scots and English forces in Ulster he decided to occupy Belfast to secure another port and get quarters for his troops.

Chichester, who commanded the English Parliamentary forces, (one of about five different factions in the country at that time) and other English officers resisted Monro's demand to occupy Belfast and Sir James Montgomery called a meeting of British colonels in Belfast on 13 May 1644, to consider whether to accept Monro as Commander in Chief. Stevenson describes the incident thus:

"There had previously been New Scots garrisoned in Belfast as well as Chichester's men, though there had been ill feeling between them but the New Scots had been withdrawn when it seemed they were going to leave Ireland. Monro's officers had demanded that they be replaced, since they did not trust Chichester to hold the town in their interests. But Chichester refused and began to fortify the town. In these circumstances Monro felt obliged to act; if he had not, his officers threatened to act on their own. A force was therefore sent from Carrickfergus which seized Belfast without bloodshed on 14th May . . . After Monro occupied Belfast the commons 'all except a very few' took the covenant. They further defied the town's superior, Chichester, by demanding changes in their constitution that all have votes in electing burgesses and that all burgesses swear the covenant."

So apart from the Scottish troops there seems to have been an important element of the population in favour of the Covenant and democratic processes.

It was presumably from this element and the Scots troops that according to Adair:

"a supplication was received by the Presbytery from many in Belfast for erecting a Session there and it was recommended to Mr. (William) Adair to do so — which was done in July 1644."

According to Benn (8) Thomas Theaker, Sovereign of Belfast, included the following statement in his deposition made on 14 July 1644 to the Commissioners in Dublin collecting evidence of the atrocities in the 1641 rebellion:

"since the Scots possessed themselves of Belfast they have erected a Presbytery there consisting of about twenty Elders and fower Deacons and have silenced Mr. Brice and other ministers in the Scottish quarters for not taking the covenant."

However Adair apparently considered Belfast weak in the faith at this time, for he comments:

"the place where there was the greatest hazard of spreading the errors of Independency and Anabaptism was Belfast — through one Matthews and one Lees being so industrious there — upon which the Presbytery recommended it to Mr. Hugh McKail and Mr. W. Cockburn (Commissioners sent over by the General Assembly in Scotland) that they might visit Belfast frequently for obviating this infection."

In 1645 some thirteen ministers were brought over from Scotland including Anthony Shaw who settled in Belfast in 1646.

The Presbytery was active at this time in attempting to establish presbyterian dominance over all other forms as evidenced by an incident described by Adair when some ministers from the Route complained to the civil authority against the Presbytery:

"The Parliament of England, having, in October 1645, sent over commissioners to Ulster to rule the affairs of this country viz. Mr. Annesley (later Earl of Anglesea), Sir Robert King and Colonel Beal, these ministers (Messrs Fullerton, Watson, Vesey and McNeil) applied to them accusing the Presbytery of bringing a foreign jurisdiction against the laws of Ireland and that the Presbytery took on them to exercise authority over them etc."

The Commissioners met the Presbytery in Belfast and supported the Presbytery:

"Here (Belfast) the commissioners sat in Presbytery; the Presbytery was encouraged and countenanced; and the others dismissed without satisfaction"

and further:

"They also did give a right to the tythe of parishes to as many new entrants as did apply to them."

These relatively good relations with the representatives of the English Parliament lasted until 1648. Adair records that in the autumn of that year:

"The Presbytery, also, upon every necessary occasion did keep correspondence with Colonel Monck (now commander of Parliamentary forces in east Ulster) and Sir Charles Coote (commander in west Ulster) and had their fair promises for concurring in settling presbyterial government in their quarters, and restraining irregular ministers of the old Conformists who acted without subordination to the Presbytery, and also some private men who were venting errors of Independency and Anabaptism. Colonel Monck's professions may appear by the letter returned in answer to divers demands of the Presbytery, as well as those of Sir Charles Coote by his letter."

The Presbytery appointed a committee consisting of Archibald Ferguson, Patrick Adair and Anthony Shaw, along with three elders to consider these letters, no doubt feeling very satisfied about the co-operation of Monk and Coote; but this favourable state of their fortunes collapsed as a result of two events in England, the defeat of the Scots army at Preston and the expulsion of the presbyterians from Parliament in Pride's purge in December 1648. The subsequent trial and execution of the King led to the bitter outburst against Parliament in the "Necessary Representation" made by the Presbytery at Belfast on 15th February 1649. Colonel Monk and Sir Charles Coote were much annoyed by the Representation and relations between them and the Presbytery rapidly deteriorated. Not only did they forbid any further administration of the Covenant, but Monk seized Carrick-fergus and sent General Monro as a prisoner to England. Lord Montgomery also deserted the Covenant having accepted a commission from Ormond (commander of the Royalist forces in Ireland) which he revealed after treacherously seizing Belfast in June 1649 and expelling Colonel Wallace, the governor of Belfast who was an elder in the presbyterian congregation. It was on this occasion that:

"Mr. Anthony Shaw, then minister of Belfast did, with great zeal and ministerial authority, upbraid the Lord of Ards before his officers."

But according to Reid, Shaw was forced at this time to retire to Scotland.

Belfast was retaken for Parliament in the autumn of 1649 by Venables who was sent north by Cromwell with a force after the seige of Drogheda when, according to Colles (9)

"800 Scots were afterwards turned out of the town"; so the congregation must then have been greatly depleted if not entirely dispersed. Venables offered to leave the presbyterian ministers unmolested if they would refrain from condemning Parliament as an illegal power, as shown by his letter of 16 June 1650, to Mr. Ferguson and Mr. Kennedy quoted by Reid:

"Whereas the ministers of the county of Down and Antrim have been summoned in a fair way before me, and have some jealousies and suspicions, as I conceive, that I intended by that summons to have entrapped them, and to have taken advantage of them had they come; this is to assure them that if they come and give me under their hand that they will not, for time to come, in their sermons and prayers, nor in other private conferences with the people, move them to sedition or trouble, or touch upon any other thing of state-matters than what is allowed by the state of England, that they shall have free liberty to depart from me again to their several places of abode and charges, and to use their ministerial functions. And that although at their being with me they shall not be convinced to give this engagement, yet if they engage that they will depart this province and repair to Scotland within ten days, they shall have free liberty to do the same."

Presbytery argued that though Ireland was subject to the King of England yet they had a Parliament of their own which had made no Acts against the King or Lords. They also reminded Venables that when he first came to Ireland he said he was come only against malignants and for the support of godly ministers but now things were quite contrary. Adair comments:

"yet the result of it was, that since they (i.e. the presbyterians) would not carry themselves submissively to the present government, they must be gone, and that they could expect no favour . . . ."

Some returned to Scotland but:

"those that stayed in the country though they could not exercise their ministry orderly as formerly, and though their stipends were sequestered yet changing their apparel to the habit of countrymen, they frequently travelled to their own parishes, taking what opportunity they could to preach in the fields or in barns and glens, and were seldom in their own houses".

A few ministers who recognised the government joined with some army chaplains in an attempt to effect a reconciliation with the remnants of Presbytery, arranging a meeting at Antrim in March 1652 at which a public debate took place, but this did not result in any change.

A note included by Young (10) dated 4 September 1652 among correspondence between the Council in Dublin and Commissioners in Belfast but not attributed to either includes:

"We are creditably informed that one Cunningham, a minister at Broad Island, hath been observed to use a passage in his prayers to this effect 'Lord wilt though give the whip into our hands again, and thou shalt see how we will scourge these enemies of thy people' and that the Scotch ministers do preach as violently against the Parliament as ever."

In October 1652 the Parliamentary Commissioners again met these ministers in Belfast but they still refused to recognise the government. The Commissioners then proposed that the ministers send two of their number to discuss matters with Lord General Fleetwood in Dublin. Archibald Ferguson and Patrick Adair were appointed for the mission but this meeting also failed to change the ministers' minds.

In 1653 Commissioners were sent north from Dublin to offer the "Engagement" — an undertaking devised by the Rump Parliament to support the government without King or House of Lords, not to be confused with the Engagement between the King and Scottish Parliament in 1647. The Commissioners sent parties of soldiers through the country to search the ministers' houses for papers and to bring these and the ministers to Carrickfergus. The only paper found was a copy of the Representation found with Mr. Adair; but this damaging document was recovered from the sergeant's cloak bag during the night and returned to Mr. Adair by a sympathetic maid. The ministers were held at Carrickfergus and though threatened with deportation to England they still refused to take the Engagement. Suddenly they were released and merely warned to live peaceably and preach the gospel. This unexpected turn of events followed Cromwell's dismissal of the Rump Parliament in April 1653, which was the body which had devised the Engagement.

A plan was now proposed to transplant some of the more difficult Scottish settlers, including ministers, to County Tipperary in order to dilute their influence in the north. Writing about this plan in April 1653 to the government in Dublin the Commissioners in Belfast state:

"In our observation of the temper of the people, we find that they are more or less perverse, according to the temper of their respective ministers, and their being planted all together or mixed among the English and Irish, which are also further arguments for us for their plantation."

The implication of this observation was that the Scots were less troublesome when mixed with English and Irish. It is interesting to note that one of the conditions to be offered to those being transplanted was:

"To that by them desired, that they be freed from subscriptions and oaths, we declare it is our principle, and (we trust) the Lord will enable us to make it our practice to use all tenderness to tender consciences."

in an order signed by Fleetwood and others in July 1653. This plan was not pursued as Cromwell, now in power, preferred other methods and was not in favour of forcing any engagement or promise upon people contrary to their conscience "knowing that forced obligation of that kind will bind no man" (Adair).

Fleetwood abandoned the policy of coercion though he still tried to win over the presbyterians, but without success. Adair records this tribute to Fleetwood:

"The truth is, that except for his delusion with the Anabaptist principles which then bore sway in the army, he seemed to be a person of great candour, and of good inclinations in the main. These good qualities I have borne witness to from experience of them; besides, I have the same from the testimoney of other judicious persons who knew him better."

Adair was obviously surprised to find good qualities in anyone holding liberal religious views.

In 1655 Fleetwood was replaced as Lord Lieutenant by Cromwell's younger son, Henry, who came, according to Adair, with "his father's instructions for moderation to all who professed the Protestant religion." Henry continued Fleetwood's policy of cooperation with the presbyterians. Among other matters he attempted to arrange stable incomes for ministers though they hesitated to co-operate even in this measure. Henry and his Council had appointed days for public fasts and thanksgiving in support of the government but the presbyterians refused to observe them "knowing (in Adair's words) that this government was iniquity at the bottom." Henry was, not unnaturally, annoyed that his efforts for friendship were thus spurned. The more lenient policy led to an increase in the number of presbyterian ministers; according to Stevenson "in 1653 it was estimated that there were twenty four presbyterian ministers in Ulster; a few years later there were nearly eighty."

Belfast did not have a presbyterian minister during this period. Gordon (11) mentions Read as having been in Belfast at this time but there is no definite information about him. Young (10) quotes a letter from the Council in Dublin to Venables in 1651:

"We have sent Mr. Wyke, a minister of the Gospel and a man of meek spirit as far as we can discern to preach the gospel in the North."

He was to be located in Lisburn and Belfast. (Adair refers to him as Mr. Weeks in his account of the debate at Antrim in March 1652). In a list of payments to ministers in 1656 given by Young, Essex Digby and William Dix are listed under Belfast. They were apparently Baptists or Independents. Whether they were acceptable to the people or whether the presbyterian element in the town had not recovered sufficiently to insist on a minister with stronger presbyterian leanings is not clear. However, this phase was brought to an end by Cromwell's death in 1658 and by the growing movement, strongly supported by the presbyterians, for the restoration of the monarchy. According to Adair, some army officers rallied the old loyalists around Dublin and in concert with loyalists in England and Scotland seized power in Dublin, sending the heads of the sectaries, who supported the Commonwealth, back to England. The presbyterians approved of this action.

Since the Irish parliament had been defunct for many years a Convention was called to meet in Dublin at the end of February 1660. This Convention consisted mainly of episcopalians though it had some presbyterian members and it appointed a presbyterian minister — Mr. Samuel Cox or Cocks — as chaplain. The Convention appointed a committee of eight ministers to advise them on matters of religion. One of these was the Rev. Patrick Adair who had instructions from his brethren in the north to secure the renewal of the Covenant. This committee drew up a list of ministers then in Ireland who were judged to be sober, orthodox men numbering almost 100 besides over 60 belonging to the Presbytery in the North.

However at this juncture the Long Parliament in England was dissolved and Monk brought home the King without any condition for religion or the Covenant. When the Cavalier Parliament met at Westminster it repudiated the King's Declaration at Breda, on which the presbyterians had set great store, and proceeded to restore the episcopate. This caused a radical change in the attitude of the convention in Dublin which dismissed the committee of eight ministers and sent commissioners to the King desiring the restoration of episcopal government and worship in Ireland.

The Presbytery met in Ballymena in the summer of 1660 in an atmosphere of considerable apprehension, for although Patrick Adair had brought back with him from the Commissioners in Dublin a warrant for each of them for tithes, the warrants were only valid for two years until bishops were appointed. The Presbytery decided to make direct representations to the King and prepared an address reminding the King of the loyalty of the Ulster presbyterians to him (and his father) in his difficult times and of his promises to resist prelacy. The two ministers appointed for this mission were William Keyes, an Englishman who had recently been appointed to Belfast and William Richardson of Killyleagh. When they reached London, Sir John Clotworthy (later Lord Massareene) who had frequently befriended the presbyterians, arranged for them to meet those close to the King; but they were advised that any protest against prelacy would be unacceptable to the King since he had already agreed to the appointment of bishops in Ireland as well as in England. The delegates persisted and after great difficulty managed to see Monk, now Duke or Albermarle, a very powerful figure, but he also advised them to amend their address omitting references to the Covenant and prelacy.

Eventually, with great reluctance, they agreed to amend the address as advised. They then gained audience with the King, and Mr. Annesley who accompanied them read the address to his Majesty. The King received it favourably and "gave them good words" referring to their constant loyalty during the Commonweath and promising protection in the future. Although Messrs Keyes and Richardson were warmly welcomed by Presbytery on their return for their success in gaining audience with the King (since other deputations from other parts of Ireland on like missions had been unsuccessful), yet the Presbytery was displeased with the amendments to the address.

Of the restored bishops three were particularly opposed to the presbyterians viz. John Bramhall formerly Bishop of Derry and now Primate, Jeremy Taylor Bishop of Down and Connor and Robert Leslie (son of old Leslie of Down) Bishop of Raphoe. When the bishops met in Dublin their first step, according to Adair, was "to procure the justices to issue forth a proclamation discharging all presbyterian meetings". The Presbytery sent four ministers to meet the Justices to remind them of the loyal stance of the Presbyterians during the Commonwealth and of the King's promise of protection. But in Council "they were reviled and mocked by the Episcopal party in Dublin and the substance of their desires was not granted."

The Bishop of Down now called on the presbyterian ministers to attend his visitation. They sent four of their number to tell him that they could not attend, not recognising episcopal authority, but that they were willing to meet him privately for discussion. Taylor would have none of it; he made it clear that he would not tolerate a presbyterian form of church government (irrespective of what attitude might be adopted in other parts of the kingdom) and declared vacant thirty six churches whose ministers were not, in his view, properly ordained. Curates were appointed to these congregations. Similar, though less drastic action was taken by other bishops and Reid gives a list of 61 ministers deposed from five northern presbyteries. Both William Keyes and Patrick Adair are on this list.

The Irish Parliament was called to meet in Dublin in May 1661 and Archbishop Bramhall was chosen to be chairman of the House of Lords. Colles (9) quotes from a letter written by Orrery to Ormond which contains this passage:

> "His Majesty having empowered the Lords Justice to appoint a fit person to be Speaker of the House of Lords, my Lord Chancellor has proposed to us the Lord Santry, against whom we had several objections . . . he being at best a cold friend to the declaration; which made me propose my Lord Primate . . . a constant eminent sufferer for His late and now Majesty, and in that choice we might let the dissenters and fanatics see what we intend as to church government."

This Parliament granted pardons to many factions who had formerly been active against the King but, reports Adair sadly "there was no mercy to presbyterians but the law was ordered to be executed against them." Once more the Presbytery sent a deputation of three of their number to petition Parliament in Dublin again reciting their loyalty to the King and his promises to them but they were not allowed to present their petition.

At this time two young ministers came over from Scotland and proceeded, with more zeal than discretion, to stir matters up in a way that embarrassed their more sober brethren and attracted unwelcome attention from the authorities. One of these ministers was Michael Bruce, great-great grandfather of Dr. Wm. Bruce of First Church. Pressure on the presbyterians was lifted in 1662 when the justices were replaced by the Duke of Ormond as Lord Lieutenant to whom Lord Massareene made representations on their behalf. But a new misfortune now befell them; Thomas Blood, formerly a Cavalier officer, came to Ireland at this time and embraced the presbyterian forms. His brother-in-law, Mr. William Lecky, was a presbyterian minister near Dublin and they, with some old Cromwellians, conceived the idea of seizing power in Dublin and overthrowing the bishops. They anticipated support from the northern presbyterians and came north for discussions with Mr. Greg, Mr. Stewart and Captain Moor. But these gentlemen flatly refused to have any part in this plot, and the presbyterians in Armagh, whom they also approached, likewise refused to become involved. Blood and Lecky pressed on with their plan in spite of this lack of support, but the Duke got intelligence of the plot and its timing and apprehended the main leaders, except

Blood, in May 1663. Although the northern presbyterians had refused to be involved in this plot they were suspected of being in support partly because of the recent presence in Dublin of the ministers attempting to present the petition and parly because the authorities had learned of the visit by Blood and Lecky to the North.

In the following month, June 1663, all the ministers who could be located were apprehended. The Antrim ministers were taken to Carrickfergus where they were held in loose and not too uncomfortable custody while the Down ministers were incarcerated at Carlingford under strict and spartan conditions. Although no evidence against them was found, suspicion was so strong that the Duke ordered that they be given the choice of quitting the kingdom or going to prison. Most of them went to Scotland; a few such as Mr. Adair were able to arrange through influential friends to stay in comparative freedom, but some were imprisoned. One of these was William Keyes of Belfast who was sent to Galway gaol. He was released upon bonds after March 1664.

So presbyterian fortunes had sunk to a low ebb, but they revived again. Bramhall died in 1663 and it gradually became clear to the authorities that the northern presbyterians had not been involved in Blood's plot so the restrictions on them were gradually relaxed. Commenting on this Adair says:

"and by degrees attained to such freedom that, in the year 1668, they began in divers places to build preaching houses, and there met publicly and performed all ordinances in a public way."

He adds that they held their monthly meetings where they began to revive discipline bringing "scandalous persons" before the Session or Presbytery. Gordon (11) assumes that Belfast was one of the "divers places" where they built a meeting house and suggests that it was located near the north gate at the junction of North Street and Hercules Street (later Royal Avenue).

The accession of the Catholic James II caused dismay among the presbyterians in Belfast so they hailed his expulsion and the accession of William and Mary with renewed hope. Patrick Adair (now minister in Belfast) and John Abernethy were delegated by the northern ministers to wait upon William to congratulate and encourage him. They brought back a letter from William to Schomberg (then quartered at Lisburn) granting protection to presbyterians. In June 1690 when William arrived in Belfast a deputation of ministers and elders led by Patrick Adair met him and he later instructed Christopher Charlton, Collector of Customs at the port of Belfast, to pay £1200 per year to Patrick Adair and six other ministers for distribution among the presbyterian ministers as a Royal Bounty (Regium Donum).

This was not the first payment to presbyterian ministers out of public funds. The early ministers who came over received tithes irrespective of their mode of ordination though sometimes the tithes were sequestered or otherwise unavailable because of disturbances. Adair mentions that the English Parliamentary Commissioners who met the Presbytery in Belfast in 1646 "gave a right of the tythe of parishes to as many new entrants as did apply to them." Then in 1649 the tithes were sequestered. Adair says:

"Those few who were left in Ireland, beside their hazard from their persecutors, and may other inconveniences, had nothing allowed them for full five years (from 1649 till 1654), except what the people under the burdens and oppressions of strangers, could, out of their poverty, spare them."

In a letter from the Council of State in 1652 it is ordered:

"that the Commissioners of Revenue in the Province of Ulster do take care that no minister within the said Province, except such as have or shall take the Engagement enjoined by Parliament, be permitted to enjoy the benefit of any tithes or of any ecclesiastical promotions or maintenance from the State."

When application was made to Fleetwood in 1654 to remove the sequestration the Council decided instead to pay them salaries out of the Treasury. The ministers did not welcome this proposal though the salaries proposed would have amounted to more than tithes in most parishes, because they would then be under an obligation to the Government. However they finally agreed and got salaries for two years. Payments made in 1656 are given by Young (10).

Later, Henry Cromwell proposed a reorganisation of parishes so that each minister would get at least £100 per year but this proposal was never fully carried out. The last occasion on which presbyterian ministers received tithes was apparently in 1660 when Patrick Adair brought back from Dublin warrants for each minister for tithes for two years until bishops were appointed. No doubt they ceased after 1661 in the case of the deposed ministers and then when, a few years later the presbyterians began to build their own meeting houses, they were presumably precluded from tithes. It was, no doubt, this circumstance which led to Sir Arthur Forbes making representation on their behalf to

Charles II as a result of which he granted them £600 out of the secret service in 1672. Reid (4) thinks this payment was made in only one year.

Regium Donum granted by William was withdrawn by Queen Anne in 1714 on the advice of the House of Lords but restored by George I in 1718 when the grant to the Synod of Ulster was increased by £400 with another £400 for the Southern Association. By 1784 the Synod of Ulster received £2,600 which was increased to £5,000 in 1792 when an attempt was being made to weaken presbyterian support for the United Irishmen. In 1803 Castlereagh increased the amount further but now congregations were classified according to size and payments fixed at £100, £75 and £50. Dr. Bruce was credited with having helped Castlereagh to devise this plan and in his letter of resignation from active ministry in 1831 he stated that he had had the First Church classified as a "collegiate" charge at this time so that a second minister, if appointed, would also receive £100 Regium Donum. Regium Donum came to an end under the Church Disestablishment Act of 1869 when the Government offered to commute annual payments to existing beneficiaries.

It is difficult in modern times to understand why the King or Government should have contributed towards the maintenance of ministers. In those days the church was an important channel of communication between the ruler and the ruled. Provision was made in the tithe system for the maintenance of a national church but when the form of the national church could not be agreed and splinter churches were formed there was a case for the ruler to attempt to maintain in these churches a co-operative attitude towards the state; to make them part of the state machine even if, on theological grounds, they did not recognise the King as head of their church.

The presbyterians were greatly encouraged by William's attitude and more ministers came over from Scotland to fill vacant pulpits and establish new congregations. It is thought that the Belfast congregation moved to Rosemary Street at this time — Gordon puts it about 1695 — but there are no existing records to confirm this date. Whether due to the influx of new blood from Scotland or a desire to appear as sound in the faith as the Episcopal Church is not clear, but in 1698, the Synod of Ulster which had been formed in 1693, resolved that in future all licentiates for the ministry would be required to subscribe the Westminster Confession of Faith. This was extended in 1705, following the Sacramental Test Act of 1704, to apply to any minister being ordained who had not previously subscribed the Confession. This step is also attributed to the preaching and subsequent prosecution of Emlyn, an Arian, for blasphemy, in Dublin in 1703.

Irish presbyterians were destined to suffer a further period of oppression during the reign of Queen Anne (1702-14) to be relieved only by the accession of George I. In addition to the disabilities caused by the Test Act (which required communion in the established church as a prerequisite to public office) they were required to take the Oath of Abjuration concerning the claims of the Pretender. McBride, who succeeded Adair as minister in Belfast, was forced to flee on several occasions because he refused to take this oath on the grounds that he could not personally know that the Pretender was not the son of James II and might therefore have a legitimate claim to the throne. It was on one of these occasions that the arresting officer pierced McBride's portrait with his sword on finding him gone. This portrait still hangs in the Session Room.

Until 1708 the presbyterians in Belfast were accommodated in one congregation but because of increasing numbers a second congregation was formed in that year; the original then becoming the First or Old Congregation. Neither of these congregations was happy about the Synod's requirement to subscribe the Westminster Confession, and when Samuel Haliday was called to the First Congregation in 1719 he refused to subscribe. He said his refusal was not based on disagreement with the content of the Confession but on the principle that no human creed should be imposed on minister or congregation. Subscription now became an important issue and those members of the two congregations who supported subscription seceded and formed the Third Congregation in 1722, which also had its meeting house in Rosemary Street until bombed in the Second World War. It is now the Rosemary Presbyterian Church in Circular Road. In 1725 all the non-subscribing congregations were placed in the Presbytery of Antrim. This Presbytery remained associated with the General Synod for another year but in 1726 was given the status of a Synod for itself and excluded in order that Synod business might "proceed peacefully."

After 1725 subscription to the Westminster Confession in the Presbyteries connected with the Synod of Ulster was again "more honoured in the breach than in the observance". Woodburn (12) says:

"In the majority of Presbyteries for the last fifty years (i.e. prior to 1830) it was not compulsory to sign the Confession at ordination and students were usually licensed without any question as to their beliefs. Only five of the fourteen Presbyteries in the Synod made subscription imperative. These were Dromore, Belfast, Route, Tyrone and Dublin."

The natural revulsion which many felt towards some of the terms of the Confession was reinforced by John Wesley's preaching and many Calvinistic Presbyterians were now Arminians, believing that salvation was offered to all and not just a few elect.

The controversy over Catholic emancipation in the early nineteenth century again split the Synod. Since 1798 an increasing number of protestants had become apprehensive about the consequences of placing political power in the hands of the Catholic majority. This faction in the Synod was led by Dr. Henry Cooke and he attacked the liberal element led by Dr. Montgomery using subscription to the Westminster Confession as the vehicle for his attack. The technique of giving political problems a religious connotation and thus removing them from the arena of rational debate was well developed in Ireland and it was used with decisive effect on this occasion. Montgomery and his followers withdrew from the General Synod and formed the Remonstrant Synod of Ulster in which freedom from "man-made" creeds was the basic tenet. The First Church was obviously sympathetic towards Montgomery who was a member of this congregation as well as minister at Dunmurry. In October 1828 the committee unanimously agreed to accede to a request from Mr. Montgomery for the use of the meeting house for a meeting of ministers and lay gentlemen who were dissatisfied with the late proceedings of the Synod of Ulster, and they granted the meeting house for the inaugural meeting of the Remonstrant Synod in 1830.

The rift between the Synods was further deepened a few years later when the General Synod adopted subscription without qualification, enabling it to join with the Seceders to form the General Assembly, thus preventing for the time being at least any prospect of reassociation with the more liberal non-subscribers. In 1835 the different non-subscribing bodies in Ireland i.e. the Presbytery of Antrim, the Synod of Munster and the Remonstrant Synod joined together to form the "Association of Non-Subscribing Presbyterians", who in 1910 came together with other liberal congregations (mainly Unitarian) to form the

Non-Subscribing Presbyterian Church of Ireland.

The First Presbyterian Church in Rosemary Street has played a leading part in all these developments, its members being prominently identified with movements which sought to sustain the individual against institutional oppression irrespective of its source.

Part of one of the massive roof trusses   Photo: Philip McConnell

CHAPTER 2 CONGREGATIONAL PROPERTY

GROUNDS

It is not clear from the records where or when the first presbyterian church was built in Belfast and there are differences in the dates and sites suggested by the various sources. Mr. G.K. Smith, congregational secretary, speaking at the centennial celebration in 1983 said:

"it was in 1642 that a church of the Presbyterian order was formed in Belfast . . . Previous to the Restoration the congregation worshipped in the Parish Church in High Street long the only 'Publique Meeting Place att Belfast'. Ejected from this place by Jeremy Taylor in 1661 they built for themselves about 1668 a house of worship, which tradition places near the North Gate i.e. at the junction of North Street and the present Royal Avenue. About 1695 the present site in Rosemary Street was obtained from the Earl of Donegall through the influence of the Rev. John McBride. On this was erected the structure taken down in 1781 and replaced by the present edifice."

Since Smith's grandfather was a member of the 1781 building committee it can be assumed that the family was well acquainted with the history of the church.

R.M. Young (13) in the *Town Book of Belfast* also gives 1642 as the year in which the First Presbyterian congregation was formed in Belfast, and other references in the record show that this had long been accepted as the correct date. The tercentenary celebration was originally planned for 1942 but after consultation with Professor Davey the committee decided that 1644 was a more appropriate date and certainly Patrick Adair's account firmly places the "erection of a Session" in July 1644 although the first Presbytery had appointed Mr. Baird to preach every third Sunday in Belfast from 1642. There is no mention of the venue to be used by Baird but he would have had three options:

1. To take over the normal service in the Parish Church and alter it a presbyterian form.
2. To hold a presbyterian form of service in the Parish Church when it was not being used for its own services.
3. To hold a service elsewhere.

The first option would have been consonant with the temper of the times, but the expression used by Thomas Theaker in his deposition in July 1644 may be thought to support the third option.

He said the presbyterians "had silenced Mr. Brice and other ministers in the Scottish quarter" which could imply a separate Scottish community with its own arrangements for religious services.

It seems likely that Anthony Shaw dominated the scene a few years later, especially in 1648 when the Parliamentary Commissioners assisted the Presbytery in "restraining irregular ministers of the old Conformists." Later, when Shaw and most of the presbyterians were turned out of the town and the Parish Church used as a military stronghold, services must have been held elsewhere. William Keyes was said to come to Belfast under the patronage of the Countess of Donegall so he may have used the Parish Church for a short time until deposed by Jeremy Taylor.

The sites for meeting houses in Belfast and dates of erection given by Smith agree with those given by Gordon in *Historic Memorials.* For evidence about the first meeting house Gordon cites an entry in the minutes of the Antrim Meeting dated 3 March 1674 that John Adam had been appointed to petition the brethren to make interest with Lord and Lady Donegall" anent the House of Worship". The meeting appointed two brethren to represent to the peer and peeress "what weighty reasons make for the people having their liberty as other congregations have, without irritation as far as possible." Gordon thinks this implies the existence of a meeting house controlled from the Castle. He refers to Thomas Philip's map of Belfast in 1685 which shows a building without chimneys at the junction of North Street and Hercules Street (Royal Avenue) which might be the meeting house. The present site on Rosemary Lane is shown as vacant on this map. R.M. Young gives 1672 as the year in which the First Presbyterian Church was erected. This date would also fit Gordon's evidence.

Gordon states that the Rosemary Lane site was obtained from Lord Donegall by McBride who became minister in 1694 and dates its use by the congregation from 1695. In the covering letter accompanying the proposals for the division of the site submitted to the Charity Commissioners by the two congregations in 1898 it is stated:

"Upwards of two centuries ago the then Earl of Donegall gave ground (which is now in the centre of Belfast) to the First Presbyterian Congregation for religious purposes upon which they erected a place of worship."

George Benn, who was a member of the congregation, gives the date of the building in Rosemary Lane as 1717 "possibly on the site of a previous structure" but it would be peculiar if a church built in 1695 had to be rebuilt so soon. When the second congregation was formed in 1708 its meeting house was erected at the rear of the First Church in Rosemary Lane so the first meeting house must have been there some time before that date.

A lease of the site was obtained from the fifth Earl, later the first Marquis of Donegall in 1767 at a rent of £1 per year but the fee simple was acquired from the Encumbered Estates Court in 1854 thus making it the absolute property of the congregation. Each congregation obtained a lease for the site of its own buildings (church and manse) while the grounds around them were held jointly by both congregations. After the Second Congregation removed to their new site and church in Elmwood Avenue in 1895 they decided to dispose of their property and interest in Rosemary Street and offered to sell them to the First Congregation. However the First Congregation decided it would not be possible to raise the necessary funds and suggested division of the common ground. A Deed of Partition dated 15.8.1899 was drawn up and agreed by the Charity Commissioners. It not only provided for the division of the common ground but empowered each congregation to dispose of its property if it so desired. The dividing wall was built in 1899 with 4½ inches on the grounds of the Second Congregation and 4½ inches plus buttresses on the grounds of the First. The First Congregation retained a right-of-way over the laneway running along the west side outside the boundary wall.

There are two references in the records to trees in the grounds; in 1803 it was agreed that one of the trees should be topped to prevent damage to Mrs. Sufferin's wall and in 1817 it was agreed that a tree should be cut down. In the annual report for 1870 it is recorded that the grounds around the church had been put in order and planted with shrubs and in May 1933 it was agreed that the shrubs in front of the church should be removed.

The site has remained substantially as it was when the lease was first obtained from Lord Donegal. Some ground was sold to the Town Improvement Committee for the purpose of widening Rosemary Street when the first Central Hall was built in 1885 and a further strip was dedicated to the Corporation in 1958 in order to straighten the frontage when the hall was being re-built. The committee considered at various times the possibility of acquiring adjoining land in order to improve the shape of this awkward triangular site but this was never accomplished. The congregation owns jointly with the Second Congregation a site at the corner of Skipper Street and Waring Street let to the Ulster

Bank Ltd., on a long lease dated 6 February 1861. These premises had been bequeathed to the two congregations by Mr. William Tennent in 1833.

Buildings: Church

Outline plans of the building which preceded the present church show it as a T shaped building with three outside staircases leading to galleries. The membership list for 1775 gives names under three "isles" viz, north, east and south and three galleries are given the same appellation suggesting that the pulpit occupied the west side. In the minutes of a meeting in October 1760 collectors for a charity sermon were allocated to the same "isles" and galleries with no mention of a west aisle or gallery. There was a session house at the north east corner of the site.

The speed with which a building committee could operate in 1781 is a matter for some envy by those who have been concerned with re-building in the twentieth century. The congregation agreed in principle to build a new House at a meeting held on 1 April 1781 but, wisely, were given a week to reflect before finally confirming their resolve at a meeting on 8 April when a building committee was appointed. Notices for these meetings were printed and delivered by the sexton to all households. The members of the building committee were: Rev. Crombie, Messrs Mattear, Maxwell, Hamilton, Smith, Thomson and Dunn. This committee met on Monday 9 April and decided to auction the materials in the old House. The advertisement was drafted and appeared in the newspaper next day and on the following Friday for auction on Saturday at 11 o'clock exactly. The material to be sold at the auction included the seats, pulpit, slates, boarded ceiling, doors and door frames and window frames and glass. Glass was to be taken away by the purchasers on the following Monday and all other materials by the end of that week i.e. thirteen days after the decision was taken to re-build. A small "earnest" was to be paid (at the auction) and three months credit given, if desired, on the remainder on approved "Notes".

On April 12 the size of the new House was agreed. It was estimated that the old House could seat 723 people (at 19 inches each) but as it was seldom more than half full it was agreed that a capacity of 600 would be sufficient. Provision was to be made for the addition of a gallery later but to be left out in the meantime. On 19 April the secretary reported that materials sold at the auction had realised £71.1.8½d. A further sale of coping, stones etc. was arranged for the end of the week and it eventually realised a further £20.8.10½d. Cross and longitudinal sections of the new House and a Bill of Scantling (quantities) prepared by Roger Mulholland were left with the chairman for inspection by any who "chuse" to propose (tender). On May 2 Mr. Dunn made the dismal report that no one had applied for copies of the sections and consequently no proposals had been made. The committee resolved "that in our opinion proposals are unlikely to be given in." This must have been a disconcerting situation for a committee which had so precipitately pulled down the old House. Notwithstanding this impasse it was decided to sell off the old walls at 2 shillings per perch in spite of Mr. Mulholland's valuation at 1 shilling 4 pence per perch. Next day agreement was reached with Roger Mulholland for the removal of the old walls.

On 12 May R. Thomson reminded the committee of previous suggestions that the new House should be elliptical in shape but the proposal had been shelved because of the problem of roofing a building of that shape. This problem had now been solved and Mr. Mulholland produced a model which was now "maturely" considered having been previously examined by members since the last meeting. In consequence it was agreed that the new House be a perfect "Ellipses" with a greater axis of 72 feet and a lesser axis of 49½ feet in the inside of the walls. The portico was to be 23 feet wide and to project 10 feet from the point of the "Ellipses". The roof was to be capped with a similar "Ellipses" 36 feet long and 13 feet wide so that all the rafters would be equally long. Since the purlines would have to be curved it was agreed that this be achieved by means of a saddle on the back of the purline rather than by cutting in sweeps which would weaken the structure. The height of the wall from the floor was fixed at 32 feet. The only proposal received for the design was one from Roger Mulholland and two members were deputed to examine the estimate in detail with him. The committee met again the following Tuesday (15 May) and ordered Mr. Mulholland to give in a new Bill of Scantling. This was ready for the next meeting on 18 May when Mr. Mulholland's estimate of £1207.10.6 was accepted. It was also agreed to cover the platform of the roof with copper which, though slightly more expensive than lead, would be lighter and more durable. (It was decided to replace the copper with lead in 1817).

The committee met again next day to agree payments to Mr. Mulholland during the work; not more than £400 to be advanced when the House was ready for the first range of windows, not more than £800 when it reached the square (i.e. top of sidewalls) and the remainder when finished but the treasurer was not to make the final payment without the approbation of the committee. Drainage of the site to the shore (drain) in Leggs Lane (Lombard Street) was also arranged together with details about plinths, cornices and the position of the House of the site. It was also resolved that the roof be covered with the best Ballywalter slates.

Building progressed rapidly, for on the 23 June the committee requested Mr. Crombie to write to Mr. Hiorne in London thanking him for his help so far, enclosing a plan of the House now under construction and requesting him to favour them with his ideas for seating. This would suggest that Mr. Hiorne might have been the author of the elliptical shape and was now being asked to solve this further problem with it. This seems more likely than the suggestion made by De Breffny and Mott (14) that the Earl of Bristol might have influenced Mulholland's selection of the oval shape.

The last recorded meeting in 1781 was on 31 July and the next record of a meeting held on 4 February 1782 opens with a note that many meetings had been held in the meantime to consider numerous plans for seating from both home and abroad but no decision had been reached. To resolve the impasse Mr. Crombie had called this meeting of the committee "with as many other gentlemen who occasionally favour us with their presence" to reach a decision. No indication is given of the author of the plan eventually agreed, but it provided for 71 pews seating 454 persons at 18 inches each (no explanation is given for allowing 1 inch less than had been used to calculate the capacity of the old House). In 1908 a sub-committee estimated the capacity of the church at 462 since which date pews accommodating 30 seats were added in the gallery and two pews with 10 seats removed, leaving a net capacity of 482 of which 316 are on the ground floor and 166 in the gallery.

The question of providing a gallery was also considered at the meeting in February 1782 and it was agreed that, "although a gallery was not required at present, it might be needed at some future date and since it could never again be put up so well so cheaply or so perfect as now," Mr Mulholland was instructed to construct bases for the pillars.

Further debate about the gallery appears to have dragged on through the summer, for it was not until 15 October 1782 that the decision to construct the gallery was finally taken. Mr. Thomson then resigned from the building committee so it seems likely that it was his opposition to it that caused the long delay in arriving at a decision. Members were invited by advertisement in the *Newsletter* to attend at the House on 28 April 1783 to fix upon their seats, and this having been satisfactorily accomplished the committee resolved on 5 May to complete the House with all possible speed. This was obviously done as it was ready for opening on 1 June 1783.

The first major alteration to the meeting house was fifty years later. On 3 June 1832 the committee had before it plans for a new portico with estimates. As so often before (and since) the committee asked for a new plan which would cost less and fixed a limit of £400. They also called for a report on any other necessary work. This report was ready by 3 August and recommended:

1. The installation of a heating system by circulating warm water in pipes
2. Re-slating the roof with superior quality large slates
3. Attention to the front, which was very dilapidated
4. Repair and repainting of windows
5. New spouting

A meeting of the congregation on 2 September decided that this work should be carried out and opened a subscription list with a target of £1200. Three weeks later the congregation met again to be told that £540 had been subscribed and £60 promised but in spite of the deficiency the decision to proceed with the work was reaffirmed.

There is no further record in the minutes of the work actually carried out at this time but it is mentioned that the Second Congregation was thanked for the use of their meeting house while the First House was closed for repair from October 1832 till March 1833. However there are references to some of the items in subsequent records. In the course of his remarks at the installation of the Rev. Alex Gordon, the Rev. J. Scott Porter said:

"In the year 1832, when I became minister . . . the Meeting-house was in a very bad condition. The roof would no longer turn off the water. The porch was in danger of falling and had to be taken down and rebuilt".

A print had been removed from the inside cover of minute book

No. 4 and under the space is the caption "front of First Presbyterian Church until November 1832" and in the vacant space is written "Print of Mg-Ho lent to M.W. & Co. 19th May '83". This is very likely the print reproduced on page 20 of "Historic Memorials" and supports the statement in the calendar for June 1944 that the portico was rebuilt in 1832. It is generally assumed that the heating system was also installed at this time. The sounding board originally located over the pulpit was removed in 1862 (presumably when the Bruce anniversary window was installed) and made into the oval table which is now in the session room, to where it was removed in 1921. Prior to that date it had been located at the front of the church and used as a communion table.

The next major alteration to the interior was in 1873 when a sub-committee consisting of E.J. Harland, F.D. Ward and G.K. Smith recommended:
1. Provision of a winding stair to the pulpit and the construction of additional pews on each side of the pulpit.
2. Construction of two pews in the southern connecting portion of the oval aisle.
3. Replacement of the windows
4. Renewal of the heating system
5. Alterations to the vestibule.

It was subsequently decided to omit alterations to the vestibule for financial reasons. A number of members obtained permission to erect memorial stained glass windows and memorial tablets at this time. A report to the commitee describing the work carried out included:
1. Stairs to pulpit remodelled and replaced and additional new pews inserted.
2. Entire windows replaced by ornamental ground glass, and stained glass memorial windows were erected by Sir Francis Hinks, John Martin, Mrs. Andrews of Ardoyne and George K. Smith.
3. Heating apparatus entirely remodelled and improved and a new boiler installed. Ventilation improved.
4. Old ceiling replaced by an entirely new and ornamental one
5. Organ rebuilt, cleaned and repaired.
6. Church cleaned and repainted

The architect for this work was Mr. Lynn; the cost was £900. In 1894 a central ventilating shaft was erected in the roof space and skylights provided. It was also agreed at this time to provide floor sheeting in the roof space to make sufficient paths to the skylights etc. but this work was not undertaken until 1980.

The next major alteration to the external appearance of the church was in 1906 when the organ chamber was constructed by Messrs McLaughlin & Harvey at the north end of the church at a cost of £770. In 1905 Mr. Alfred Hollins was consulted about the siting of the new organ being presented by the Misses Riddel and he advised the construction of an organ chamber 20 feet by 12 feet but in May 1906 the organ builders complained of insufficient room so the chamber was extended by 1 foot. During this construction work it was discovered that an old disused sewer ran obliquely under the church and that there was no proper foundation under the floor. It was also decided that the bases to the pillars supporting the gallery were inadequate and new bases were inserted. (In 1943 it was reported that these pillars had a solid metal core).

Not everyone agrees that the construction of the organ chamber was a good idea; about it Charles Brett (15) says: "Architectural purists (amongst whom I must number myself) will regret that the opportunity was not taken to move the organ and restore the full ellipse of walls and pews" i.e. during restoration in 1975. However apart from cost, which was in any case a determining factor, Mr. Hollins felt that the organ could not be placed within the ellipse for acoustical reasons and the success of the present arrangement from the musical point of view is attested to by many music lovers.

In 1933 a special fund was raised in connection with the 150th anniversary of the meeting house and used for re-pointing the external brickwork, the installation of an electric motor for the organ, the installation of radiators behind the organ and general redecoration of the church, and in 1949 new gutters and down pipes were fitted. The Architectural Heritage Society suggested to the committee in 1972 that the plaster should be removed from the portico exposing the stonework thought to have been used in its construction. This had been considered in 1949 when the estimate for removing the plaster and sand blasting the stonework was £725 but, apart from cost, the committee had grave doubts whether the quality of the stone work would be good enough for this treatment seeing that it had been plastered in 1832 when built. The name and dates of founding and rebuilding were placed over the door in 1881.

The original design and construction of this building must have been good to remain intact on an unpiled site on Belfast silt. Apart from traffic vibration, it has been subjected to vibration from other sources, notably in 1953 when the Masonic Hall site was being piled, and in 1974 a car bomb in Royal Avenue must have rocked the building on its foundations. Some minor cracks are apparent but that the walls have withstood these shocks without any sign of major disintegration is a tribute to the workmen who originally constructed them two centuries ago.

Pews

There is little information about the type of pews in the old building but they seem to have been altered from time to time by the committee or occupants as desired. A list of pew rents in 1760 refers to single and double seats. In 1771 the committee decided that vacant pews should be padlocked and the keys kept in the vestry to be given out to any who took a pew, so there must have been pew doors in the old building too. In 1773 the committee ordered that two single seats in the "North Isle" be converted to one large single seat and in 1775 it was resolved that two single seats next to the pulpit be given to Mr. John Holmes to make into one. About this time there was a long drawn out disagreement between the committee and a Capt. Stewart who had spent "upwards of six guineas repairing his own seat" and requested a refund or a lease of the seat but the committee refused to accede to either request. Apparently the Second Congregation had adopted the practice of leasing seats as their records contain reminders to members that the names and addresses of any person to whom they had sub-let should be given to the minister within one month.

The pre-occupation of successive committees with allocating and re-allocating seats suggests that pews in the church were looked upon as private property in much the same way as houses in a modern housing estate. In the first minute book seats are referred to as "possessed" by so and so, but in 1772 the committee resolved "that the granting of leases of their seats to any members would be destructive to the interests of the congregation" and in 1794 it was resolved "that in future no members may assign their seats without the committee's approbation" so apparently the committee considered it important to retain control over pew lettings. Private ownership was apparently common in other churches too for Charles Brett (16) recalls that in 1824 his ancestor advertised for sale or to let "his excellent pew, in the west gallery, St. George's Church, with cushions complete", and another example of leasing a pew in the Third Congregation in 1763 is quoted by R.M. Young in *Historical Notices of Old Belfast.*

"This indenture made the twenty-ninth day of September in the year of our Lord One thousand seven hundred and sixty three between John Clark of Belfast in the County of Antrim, on the One part, and John McCracken of Belfast aforesaid Mariner, of the other part, Witnesseth that the said John Clark for, and in consideration of the sum of eleven pounds sterling hath granted, bargained sold, aliened, released and confirmed and by these Presents doth grant . . . . and confirm to the said John McCracken in his actual possession now being: All that the Seat or Pew in the Third or new-erected Meeting House of Protestant Dissenters in the Town of Belfast aforesaid, Number (1) below stairs with the Appurtenances hereunto belonging. To have and to hold the same unto the said John McCracken his Heirs and assigns, and all and every other person or persons whatsoever, shall and will warrant and for ever defend these Presents."

It is interesting to compare with the Jewish practice as described by Isaac Levy (17):

"Another feature of the seating arrangements prevailing in the modern synagogue which claim to be established in accordance with ancient tradition, is the allocation of fixed places to regular worshippers or members. Whilst there is no record that such a practice was based on the payment of a statutory fee as is the custom in our synagogues, there is evidence that worshippers were encouraged to occupy fixed places in the synagogue . . . Although one cannot state with certainty when the practice to pay for such seats came into being, there can be no doubt that by the Middle Ages it had become firmly established and was regarded as normal to sell seats to worshippers, presumably in order to raise funds for the maintenance of the synagogues. By such transactions seats became the private property of the purchaser and could be transmitted to one's heirs as part of their inheritance . . . for whilst permanent ownership of seats may have lapsed in many congregations, though still preserved in some, the method of calculation of their value had not altered. The computation in relation to the proximity to the Ark and the east wall . . . is still a marked feature of the gradations of seat rental".

There is no record of members undertaking any alteration of pews after the new House was opened in 1783 but the private furnishing of pews with cushions, foot-rests etc., was continued until quite recent times. In 1817 the treasurer was:

"ordered to pay the upholsterer for work done in Dr. Drennan's and Mr. Moreland's seats and that the same be considered the property of the congregation these proprietors having declined to pay".

As recently as 1884 the collector of stipend was requested by the committee to make an inventory of pew furniture defining ownership as far as he possibly could and to have a special mark made on those cushions which belonged to the congregation. Again in 1896 he was authorised to purchase a cushion for a pew and directed to make an inventory of cushions belonging to the congregation, so this was a transitional period when private pew furnishing was being phased out.

Pews have been altered on several occasions since the new House was built. The original seating plan provided a continuous oval aisle parallel with the walls, but in 1872 pews were constructed in the southern end of the ellipse creating two separate curving aisles. At the same time winding stairs were provided for the pulpit and additional pews constructed on either side of it The reason given for these alterations was the need to provide sittings for the waiting list of applicants.

In 1812 "two seats were added to the front and two to the rear of each end of the gallery" and in 1908 pews were constructed in the portion of the gallery left vacant by the removal of the organ and choir to the ground floor. This change had necessitated the removal of a pair of pews at the front of the oval to make room for the organ console, and in 1956 a further pair of pews was removed to increase the space available at the front of the church for communion, weddings etc. So the original plan of seating had been fairly extensively modified over the years for functional reasons but these changes have not altered greatly the original concept of the oval shape.

During an inspection of the church in 1951 the property committee discovered woodworm infestation in the roof timbers and in the pews. This was treated on several occasions in subsequent years and is believed to have been eradicated but periodic inspections are necessary. An infestation of dry rot was found in timber in the vestry in 1975 and this also was treated and eradicated.

Heating

The first mention in the records of a proposal to heat the building artificially was in 1803 when Mr. Houston raised the question of providing stoves and was deputed to obtain estimates. Apparently no action was taken then , for in 1824 the question was again raised, but as insufficient funds were available for all the work then required the stoves were removed from the list of priorities. However a circulation system was installed eight years later in 1832; perhaps the idea of stoves was not generally acceptable   although this method of heating churches was not uncommon at this time.

Lighting

There is no direct reference in the records to the use of candles on oil lamps in the church but an article in the *Northern Whig* for 4 February 1895 speculates that candles had been used:
"The appliances throughout are very pretty, but in no place did the light show forth with better effect than from the handsome old fittings suspended along the front of the gallery which were first chandeliers: next gasaliers and now — well we find it difficult to designate them properly. They must have been somewhat imposing when they held lighted candles, they served their purpose well with gas, and apparently little trouble was required in transforming them to the use of the new illuminant".
Candles were used during a strike in 1919 as recorded in the annual report for that year:
"The local strike, by depriving us of the electric light on several Sunday evenings, caused much inconvenience, but by the use of candle-light, the continuity of the services was maintained",
and of course more recently candles have been used for the carol service.

It is difficult to fix precisely the date on which evening service commenced as the references could indicate several different times, but in 1835 the committee agreed in principle to hold evening services and appointed a sub-committee to arrange for gas light to be installed. (Gas lighting for the streets of Belfast had been introduced in 1823). Apparently this was done, for in 1837 the committee had before it a complaint about the very offensive smell "so disagreeable to those whose seats are in the gallery" arising from the use of gas lighting. This problem appears to have persisted for a long time because it was consideration of the problem of the ventilation of the house in 1894, that led the building committee to investigate the use of electricity "now that it was being adopted by the City Council".

The installation was undertaken and electric light used for the first time at evening service on 3 February 1895. It has been claimed that this was the first church in Belfast (and possibly the whole of Ireland) to be so lighted. Whether that claim is justified or not the initial installation was not very satisfactory as Messrs. Jas. Lowden & Co. of Ann Street reported to the committee in 1908 that it was the worst lighted church in Belfast:

"the ground floor is at present lighted by means of four eight light electroliers, the lamps being 16 candle power. The gallery is dealt with along each side by three 2 light fittings in addition to a couple at the back portion. On each side of the pulpit is a fitting with two lamps".

The lamps in use were referred to as carbon filament which used more current in relation to light produced than metallic filament lamps. They recommended the substitution of the latter increasing the candle power from 512 to 1024 and also the provision of an electrolier from the centre rosette of the ceiling. These improvements were apparently undertaken at that time but further changes were made in 1920 when Mr. T.H. McMurray recommended to the committee that:

"the gas fittings, which had been adapted for electric lights, should be discarded being unsuitable and interfering with the view of worshippers occupying the rear pews. The light should be uniform and all lighting units removed as far as possible from the direct vision of the congregation to achieve which they should be near the ceiling or along the outer wall".

Apparently the present central electrolier was supplied at this time and the lights under the gallery floor fitted. In March 1921 it was agreed to retain one of the sconce fittings for the session room on account of its historic value. Apparently these sconce fittings had been suspended along the front of the gallery. The church was re-wired for electricity in 1957 by Messrs Jim Meneely and Fred McMurray.

Memorials

The first memorial was the tablet to Charles Hamilton erected in the vestibule by his sisters after his premature death in 1782 (age 39). Hamilton served with Hastings in India and was an oriental scholar of some distinction. His mother was a sister of the Rev. James Mackay and one of his sisters was Elizabeth Hamilton the authoress. This memorial was originally fixed to the wall facing the main entrance but in 1922 was removed to the east side of the vestibule to make the more prominent site available for Miss Rosamund Praeger's War Memorial for those who served and died in the First World War.

The first memorial inside the church was the one erected in 1842 by the congregation in memory of the Rev. Dr. William Bruce. The arrangements for it would be recorded in the missing minute book but an entry on page 71 of the account book reads:

"The congregation having resolved at their General meeting on 18th April 1841 'That a suitable Monumental Tablet to the memory of the late Rev. Dr. Bruce be erected in the Meeting House' the same had been executed by Messrs. Robinson, Kelly & Brown from a design by Mr. Lanyon".

The subscription list opened in August 1841 and continued till November 1843. The memorial cost £70 and the design £8.8.0.

The next memorial was the stained glass window installed by the congregation in 1862 on the 50th anniversary of the ordination of the Rev. Wm. Bruce. This window was placed in the north end of the oval behind the pulpit. In 1880 the committee agreed to consult the Bruce family on a proposal to remove this window: "the same long since having been condemned as an inferior work of art" but although it is recorded that the Bruce family cordially approved the proposal, there is no further reference to it and it seems likely that the window was re-sited in the organ chamber when it was constructed in 1906. The large centre section of this window was damaged beyond repair in 1974 and was replaced by a new design but the original small side windows remain. In 1873 the Andrews, Hincks, Martin and Smith families all obtained permission to install memorial stained glass windows as did the Ward family in 1923. The Riddel memorial window, installed in 1929, was unveiled by Sir Richard Livingstone, Vice Chancellor of Queen's University.

The Patterson and Riddel families were given permission to

erect memorial tablets in 1872, and in 1880 the congregation erected memorial tablets to the Rev. Wm. Bruce and the Rev. J. Scott Porter, the medallions for which were made in Munich by Mayer & Co. The Davidson tablet was erected in 1917 and that to the seven Bruce sisters in 1933. In 1967 the congregation erected the memorial tablet to the Rev. Alexander Gordon. There is no reference in the minutes to the tablets erected to J. Holmes Houston, William Tennent, Dr. S.S. Thomson, John Martin and Alethea Maria Ferguson but in his reply to an address on the presentation of his portrait to him on 22 May 1880, G.K. Smith includes these as amongst those erected during his secretaryship. There is no reference in the records to the memorial to E.S. Mercer.

The War Memorial for members who served in the First World War was designed and executed by Miss Rosamond Praeger of Holywood and unveiled by Miss Charlotte Bruce in 1922. In 1949 Miss Praeger was consulted about adding to it the names of those who served in the Second World War and advised that they could be added, but after further consideration it was agreed that it would be more appropriate to place a tablet with their names in the new hall when it was rebuilt.

Bomb Damage

The church sustained some damage from the fire which consumed the Central Hall in the incendiary air raid on the night of 4-5 May 1941. The glass in the windows was cracked and exposed timbers were scorched along the east side of the church. However it suffered much more severe damage from car bombs during the civil disturbances in the 1970s. The church itself was not a target but five explosions in the vicinity all caused damage to the building. These were in North Street in June 1972, in Lombard Street in July 1972, in Royal Avenue in March and October 1974 and December 1975. The most severe were those in March and October 1974 which not only damaged the windows, slates etc. as did the others, but displaced the roof breaking its ties with the side walls. The ceiling was consequently damaged beyond repair and had to be completely replaced.

In spite of the daunting appearance of the church with windows missing, walls cracked, the roof badly damaged and the interior covered with dust and rubble, the committee decided that it must be restored if possible and, recognising that the severe nature of the damage called for professional assistance, appointed Messrs. Isherwood and Ellis, architects for the restoration work. It was clear that restoration would cost many thousands of pounds and was far beyond the sum which the congregation could raise. Compensation would be payable under Criminal Injuries legislation but it was stressed from the beginning that such compensation could not be expected to cover the whole cost and indeed might fall considerably short of the cost depending on the allowance made for "betterment", that is the enhanced value of the new structure due to the use of new materials and up to date techniques. This would be deducted from the total cost and compensation based on the difference. Another even more serious consideration was that major defects due to the passage of time and not attributable to bomb damage might be discovered in the course of the work. The cost of repairing such defects would have to be borne entirely by the congregation. It was therefore impossible to estimate the congregation's commitment before work commenced and it had to make the agonising decision whether to undertake an unknown commitment or abandon the church forever for, with continuing inflation, the financial gap would widen rapidly as time passed.

After many meetings and much anxious discussion the congregation decided on 6 October 1974 to undertake restoration under a contract which provided for termination of work at any stage should it become obvious that all the work needed could not be financed. At the same time it was decided to launch an appeal to meet the deficit between compensation and the cost of the work of restoration. Since the church had been listed as a building of special architectural or historic interest the congregation felt justified in addressing this appeal to bodies interested in maintaining such buildings and to the general public as well as to its own members. The appeal was well supported, over £16,000 being raised by 31 December 1978. Of this more than half was subscribed by members of the congregation and over £2,000 by Non-Subscribing and Unitarian Churches and organisations from as far afield as Australia, South Africa and the United States and including £1,500 from the John Gregson Trust. Almost £5,000 subscribed by organisations and individuals not connected with us was contributed mainly by residents and businesses in Belfast but included a substantial grant of £3,000 from the Pilgrim Trust. The congregation was particularly pleased to receive subscriptions from Roman Catholic friends. A complete list of subscriptions has been permanently recorded in the minute book.

Restoration work commenced at the end of 1974 and by 1976 the structural damage had been repaired and the ceiling replaced. This was accomplished by preparing moulds from the remains of the old ceiling and casting the new ceiling in sections with fibrous plaster. The sections were then fixed in place. The organ was cleaned and repaired in 1979, and in March 1981 the decision was taken by the congregation to commence work on replacing the stained glass windows. It had been intended originally to renew the floor and to provide the proper foundation talked about in 1906, but when this was considered it was impossible to estimate the cost of removing and replacing the old curved pews or indeed to be sure that they could be replaced at all, so it was decided to re-floor the aisles only and leave the remainder to be repaired from time to time as necessary.

Central Hall

The Central Hall stands on the site of the manse occupied by the Rev. Thomas Drennan when the earliest records commence in 1760. The Rev. Dr. Crombie resided in this manse from 1770 till 1783 when he moved to the Academy. The committee then leased the house to a Mr. Haslett. A record in the minutes in 1799 states that Joseph Wright, a solicitor, who had recently purchased Mr. Kennedy's interest in the dwelling house formerly let to Henry Haslett had applied for a renewal of the lease which had still ten years to run. The committee agreed to offer a lease for 81 years containing a covenant for rebuilding at a cost of not less than £300.

In January 1801 Joseph Wright wrote to the committee stating that he had spent a considerable sum rebuilding and repairing the premises and requesting completion of the lease. It was agreed to do so, subject to the clauses in the lease granted by the late Marquis, this lease to date from 1 November 1799 and to run for 81 years at a rent of £30 per year. There is no information about the alterations made by Mr. Wright but it seems probable that the old manse was converted into shops as shown in the water colour of the old building presented to the committee by a Mr.H. Thomas in 1885 and now hanging in the lounge. A report in the *Northern Whig* for 19 March 1885 included the phrase "There are still some who can remember the building before it was turned into shops" which might imply a more recent reconstruction

In 1824 Joseph Wright wrote to the committee requesting a review of his lease so possibly he was considering structural alterations then. The committee declined to take any action. The minutes of the committee for 9 October 1880 gives the following information about the expiring lease:

Number	Tenant	Estimated Value	Poor Law Valuation
25	Wm. Beattie & Son	£50	£33
27	Wm. Savage	£55	£30
29	Ulster Unitarian Christian Association	£50	£32

So while the committee avoided having to raise the capital required for rebuilding in 1799, they were receiving only £30 per year for premises estimated to be worth £155 per year at the end of the long lease.

From 1880 the tenancies were renewed annually until 1882 when a proposal to build a congregational hall on the site was considered. A sub-committee consisting of the Rev. A. Gordon, W. Sinclair Boyd, G.K. Smith and E.J. Harland reported in October 1882 that as a sum of £3,000 would be required to build a hall it was not considered possible. The committee accepted this view but added that they would not be averse to building a hall if the necessary funds could be raised. One suggestion at this stage was to incorporate accommodation for the congregation's day school then located in Fountain Street, but Mr. W.D. Andrews Q.C. advised the committee that the proceeds of the Fountain Street property could not properly be used for the erection of a congregational hall. However those in favour of a hall kept up the pressure; the secretary, Mr. G.K. Smith took the unusual course of writing to the committee eulogising the congregation and its role in the religious life of Belfast and strongly urging the erection of a hall. The Presbytery visited the congregation at this time and in their findings urged the provision of better accommodation for the Sunday school. The sub-committee which organised the centennial celebrations in 1883 took up the question of a hall and engendered a new enthusiasm leading to the opening of a sub-scription list on 22 July 1883 for which the treasurers were W. Sinclair Boyd and John Rogers.

By the end of the year £1,389 had been promised, so on 17 February 1884 the committee decided to demolish the old buildings and erect a hall. A building committee was appointed of which E.J. Harland was chairman and J.R. Musgrave vice-chairman. This committee appointed Mr. Fennell architect for the new building on 8 March and entered into negotiations with the Town Council for the widening of Rosemary Street, and with the Second Congregation for adjustment of the boundary of the common ground. Mr. Fennell produced plans by October 1884 but they were apparently considered too elaborate for he was asked to redesign his proposals so as to bring the cost down to about £2,000. The new plans were approved in January 1883 and tenders invited. Fourteen tenders were received and that from Robert John Kerr accepted. The old building was demolished in March 1885.

Members of the building committee suggested to Mr. Harland who was Mayor of Belfast that year, that he should lay the foundation stone but he did not approve of a public ceremony at this stage preferring that it be reserved for opening the hall, so the foundation stone was laid at a private ceremony by G.K. Smith on 8 June 1885. A report of this event in the *Northern Whig* on 9 June stated that the frontage of 64 feet had been set back 10 feet at the Lombard Street end and 2½ feet at the other to widen Rosemary Street. Three shops were to be provided on the ground floor and a hall 55 feet by 28 feet on the first floor. The elevation was to be of red brick rising to 52 feet. The first floor was to be divided into bays with grouped pilasters over which was an entablature. The upper storey was to be in bays with circular headed windows and a parapet which would conceal the roof from the street.

Suggested names for the hall considered by the committee included Centennial, Rosemary, Alexandra, Prince of Wales, Crombie, Antrim and Harland but eventually it was named the Central Hall. It cost £1,989.13.10 and was opened by Sir E.J. Harland (by then knighted) on 14 January 1886. The three shops had been let by the opening date including one to the Ulster Unitarian Christian Association. Total rents were £135 per year. The first scale of charges for the hire of the hall are interesting. They were:

religious or charitable meetings	£1.1.0
lectures or business meetings	£2.2.0
concerts or other meetings	£3.3.0

Apparently the patrons of art were considered more affluent than the business community.

As soon as agreement was reached on the division of the common ground with the Second Congregation in 1898 the committee commenced consideration of extending the hall and in 1899 requested Messrs Young & Mackenzie (architects) to prepare plans. Among the possibilities discussed was one to raise the height by one storey but Messrs Robb who owned premises on the other side of Rosemary Street warned the committee through their solicitors that they would object to any encroachment on their rights to ancient lights. A number of plans were produced and modified either because of the financial commitment or the "ancient lights" problem but eventually an additional shop (No. 41 Rosemary Street) with offices above and a minor hall at the rear were added in 1901. The lay-out of the Central Hall was also altered at this time so as to place a row of rooms between the hall and the street to reduce traffic noise in the hall. It was agreed to install electricity as well as gas in both halls. An estimate was obtained from the Sirocco Engineering Works for the installation of electric ventilation fans in both the hall and the church at £190.10.0 but it was considered too expensive.

The size of the hall was given at 55 feet by 28 feet with a seating capacity of 350 at the time of its original construction. In April 1905 the Sexton was instructed, for safety reasons, not to put out more than 200 chairs but this could be increased to 250 when the platform extension was not in use. On several occasions it was decided not to let the hall for balls or dances (1886 and 1908) though this ban was later relaxed for dances organised by congregational organisations. In 1893 there was discussion about a crack in the walls of the Central Hall thought to be associated with the piling of an adjacent site.

At the routine committee meeting on 4 May 1941 it was reported that the Domestic Mission had been destroyed in the air raid on 15/16 April and that nine members had lost their lives. York Street Church had also been damaged beyond repair. It was agreed to purchase three steel helmets for fire watchers. At a special meeting of the committee one week later (11 May) the Rev. Dr. Wilde reported on the destruction of the hall in the raid of 4/5 May. The Rev. Rowland had heard that the centre of the town (especially Rosemary Street) had been heavily attacked with incendiary bombs and went there with a German refugee (Mr. Lothar Berglas) who was staying with him and another friend, telephoning the Rev. Dr. Wilde on the way. The Rev. Wilde and his son Geoffrey arrived at the hall at 4 a.m. and found it burning fiercely with flames licking the church. They used a stirrup pump to keep the church from setting alight until an Auxilliary Fire Service crew arrived at 5.30 a.m. with a power hose saving the church and part of the minor hall. The paid firewatcher Mr. G. Patterson and the caretaker Mr. Tinsdale had vacated the premises at 2 a.m. and had not been heard of since. In the calendar for September 1943 a tribute is recorded to two Roman Catholics, Mr. Thomas Loughrey and Mr. John Hennessy, who had assisted the Rev. Rowland and Mr. Berglas to save the church but who had quietly left the scene before they had been identified, resulting in the belated acknowledgement of their vital contribution to saving the church from destruction.

The church in Rosemary Street belonging to the Third Congregation and the Congregational Church in Donegall Street had been destroyed and it was agreed to offer the use of First Church to those congregations. It was also agreed that the main organ pipes and other valuables and records should be removed for greater safety to Clough and Rademon. The lead box containing contemporary documents which had been placed in the foundations of the hall was recovered in 1943. Since there was no immediate prospect of replacing the building, arrangements were made with the War Damage Commission for temporary repairs to what remained of the minor hall so that it could be used for congregational purposes in the meantime. Compensation for the contents of the hall was also agreed at £1,470.

In April 1945 a sub-committee was formed to negotiate with the War Damage Commission for the restoration of the building. The War Damage Act provided for two forms of compensation; one was a value payment for commercial buildings in which the amount of compensation was the difference between the 1939 estimated value of the building and the value of any portion remaining undamaged, and the other a cost of works reinstatement of the original building. The latter method of compensation applied to ecclesiastical buildings which were totally destroyed. The first hurdle was to establish that the Central Hall met the criteria for an ecclesiastical building. In 1946 the Rev. Dr. Wilde prepared a detailed account of the accommodation and usage of the hall, which after consultation with Sir James Andrews, was submitted to the Commission. Mr. R.B. McCutcheon prepared plans and details of the building and after much negotiation and discussion the Commission eventually accepted in June 1949 that the Central Hall was eligible for cost of works reinstatement.

The method of calculating compensation was to prepare a bill of quantities for the old building and apply to it the prices in the contract for the replacement building (which need not be identical though it must provide substantially the same accommodation), so the amount of compensation could not be determined until plans had been made for the new hall and tenders obtained. In addition to this difficulty current building regulations required this site to be piled for a new building, but since the former building had not been piled no compensation would be available for this item estimated at about £12,000. In spite of these uncertainties the committee decided to have plans for a new hall prepared and these were produced in 1951 by Messrs Gibson & Taylor who had been appointed architects. However when the plan was costed it was estimated that the cost of building would be at least £90,000 while the estimate for War Damage compensation was about £30,000. This was obviously an impossible gap for the congregation to bridge so a fresh start had to be made. In the meantime the committee was investigating the possibility of building the shops so as to restore income, and a nissen hut to serve as a hall, but neither proved feasible.

By 1953 the architects produced a modified plan for a building two storeys high to which a further two storeys could be added later, thus achieving the original concept. It was calculated that this phase of the building would cost about £15,000 more than estimated compensation, and that income from lettings over expenses would be sufficient to pay off the loan required over a twenty-year period. These estimates depended on two important assumptions about which there was considerable doubt. The first was the cost of piling; the depth required could only be established after work commenced and if deeper piles were required than was estimated the cost would rise rapidly as the cost per foot increases with increasing depth (the estimate was based on piling to a depth of 65 feet); the second assumption concerned shop rents which remained high but might be adversely affected by a post war depression such as had occurred after other wars. If one assumption proved wrong the result for the congregation would be serious; if both were wrong it would be disastrous. So work on the plans was stopped and the whole situation carefully re-examined.

The safe course to adopt would have been to accept a "value payment" for the old building and sell the site. It was estimated that this course would result in a sum of about £17,000 becoming available for investment. While favoured by a few, the great majority of the congregation urged that the hall should be rebuilt. With a view to removing some of the risk of re-building a fresh approach was made to the War Damage Commission on the question of the compensation for piling on the grounds that since the original building could not now be replaced without piling the site, this cost should be included for compensation. The Commission could not concede this argument but, appreciating the dilemma in which the congregation was placed, they pointed out that if a building could be planned which substantially replaced the old hall and be built for a lower cost than would be required for identical reinstatement, the savings could be devoted towards the cost of piling. This line of thought led the committee to propose a three or four storey building on a part of the site designed to just replace the accommodation which would attract full compensation but reduce the area to be piled.

The architects were briefed afresh along these lines and produced a new sketch plan by May 1955 which was approved by the congregation. The revised plan was then submitted to the War Damage Commission and accepted by them in January 1956 as substantially replacing the old hall. This plan was costed at £36,000 and so was much closer to the estimated compensation. A firm decision was taken to erect this building though a few members, including the hon. treasurer who resigned the treasurership, considered the risk still too great for a small congregation to undertake. The majority, while apprehensive, were determined to go ahead with the building. Tenders were invited in the summer of 1957 and ten firms had tendered by the closing date on 10 August. The amounts ranged from £42,170 to £49,094. By November the revised estimates based on contract prices were ready and these showed a total building cost of £51,000 and compensation at £37,000. The congregation reaffirmed its decision to go ahead with the building and agreed to launch an appeal with a target of £10,000.

On 22 February 1958 the hon secretaries and the newly appointed treasurer signed the contract with Messrs. Jas. Buckley & Sons Ltd., of Belmont Road. The Deeds for all the congregation's property were lodged with the Ulster Bank Ltd., against a possible overdraft. There were still some unknowns; the depth of piling required was still an estimate and, as was customary in post-war conditions, the terms of the contract provided for increases due to rising costs. It was with mixed feelings that the officers committed themselves and the congregation to an enterprise of this magnitude carrying quite significant risks, particularly as the War Damage Commission had only committed itself to £29,000 in a letter early in February, subject to the addition of a number of other items still to be negotiated and calculated.

In the summer of 1958, piling was completed within the estimate and the appeal which had been launched was generously supported by members and friends not only in Ireland but abroad, so it was in a much more optimistic mood that arrangements were made for a ceremony on 6 September 1958 at which Miss A.M. McKisack laid the foundation stone and the Rev. Dr. McLachlan a stone commemorating the former hall. Construction occupied the next year and the opening ceremony, at which the Rt. Hon. J.L.O. Andrews M.P., opened the hall and unveiled the War Memorial, took place on 7 November 1959. Visitors at this ceremony included the Right Rev. H.C. Elliott, the Rev. Dr. Davey, the Right Rev. J.W. Dyer, Mr. A.L. Blake, Rev. Donald Cairns, Mrs. Douglas, Mr. Peskett and Mrs. Taggart. During the ceremony the first solo in the hall was, appropriately, sung by Madame Eileen Ervine.

Compensation had not been finalised when the hall was opened and because of the uncertainty about the financial outcome it was decided to defer the installation of the lift in the meantime. However many people were anxious that it should be completed as soon as possible. In the summer of 1960 the committee received two substantial anonymous gifts towards the lift, one for £1,000 from "interested ladies" and another for £500. This enabled the committee to go ahead with the lift which was installed early in 1961. The final financial figures were:—

Cost of Building:

Payment to Contractors	£48,877. 9. 9
Furnishing	2,303.18.1
Professional Fees	6,308. 6. 5
Printing Appeal literature	87.11.0
	£57,577. 5. 3

Funds available:

Balance in building fund 1958	£5,452.17.4
£10,000 Appeal	10,683.11.9
War Damage Compensation	38,708. 0. 7
Transfer from revenue	1,500. 0. 0
	£56,344. 9. 8

So the time which had been spent in agonising discussion and argument was not wasted; it all contributed to this very satis-factory outcome. Although the new hall was a three-storey building, the piles and steel-work were designed for four storeys so that another could be added, if required, at a future date. The list of subscribers to the rebuilding fund has been permanently recorded in minute book No. 16.

In 1965 the old minor hall was demolished and the area surfaced to facilitate car parking. An agreement was made with the Masonic authorities for the use of their right-of-way from the end of the congregation's own right of way at the north east corner of the perimeter to an opening made in the wall at the rear. In 1966 the main kitchen in the hall was extended by incorpor-ating part of the men's cloakroom which was moved to the mezza-nine floor. The Ulster Unitarian Christian Association had been unable to rent the smallest shop in 1959. It became vacant in 1966 and was offered again to the Association at a nominal rent but consideration of the costs and possible returns indicated that such an enterprise would not be feasible.

Manses

There is no reference to any manse having been provided for the early ministers of the congregation. The first such reference is in the Deed by Lord Donegall in 1767 in which the site of the meeting house and a manse was granted to the congregation. This manse was on the south east portion of the site fronting on to Rosemary Street. According to an article in the *Northern Whig* of 19 March 1885, this house had been erected at the beginning of the eighteenth century and was first occupied by McBride (who came to Belfast in 1694) and the last minister to occupy it was Crombie who moved out of it to the Academy in 1783. An inter-esting account is given in the first minute book of how it was allocated. The committee decided to leave Mr. Mackay and Mr. Crombie to decide between themselves which of them should occupy it but should they both desire to live in it they were to cast lots. It is not recorded which method was used. The *Whig* article referred to above mentions that amongst those born in this manse were Dr. Haliday and Dr. Drennan of United Irishmen fame.

This house, having been let on a long lease in 1799, was not available for the Rev. Wm. Bruce when he was ordained in 1812 nor for the Rev. Dr. Bruce when he gave up the Academy in 1823. The Rev. Wm. Bruce lived at 10 Wellington Place for a time but built "The Farm" in 1834. Scott Porter lived at 16 College Square East though his funeral in 1880 was from Lennoxvale. Apparently the house in College Square had been given to him by the congregation for in reply to a testimonial on the presentation of his portrait to him in College Square in 1873 he said "in requital of my humble, but well meant exertions (a reference to his debate with the Rev. Bagot in 1834) I was presented with the lease of this and the adjoining house". The Rev. Alex Gordon had an address at 9 Lower Crescent, the Rev. J. Kirk Pike at Wynstay, Rosetta Park and the Rev. Douglas Walmsley at Redburn, Adelaide Park.

In the annual report for 1875 it is recorded that Andrew Kirk, Marsden Villa, Antrim Road, Belfast, provided in his will for a number of substantial bequests including one for a manse for the First Presbyterian Church. In 1906 it was discovered (through a misdirected letter) that the Third Congregation had claimed this legacy, but in a subsequent court action in Dublin it was established that it was intended for the First Church. The total amount which had accrued by that time was over £1200 and the congregation purchased the house in Cadogan Park for £790, using the balance to purchase the freehold from Mr. Workman a few years later. The name was changed from "Markinch" to "Ardeevin" (meaning, in Irish, beautiful height), selected from a number suggested. The Rev. H.J. Rossington was the first minister to occupy this manse.

This large house, built at a time when domestic servants were customary, became too difficult to maintain as a family residence and proposals to sell it and purchase a smaller house were considered from time to time. Eventually action was taken in 1976 when, apart from the expense of modernisation needed, the house was much too big for the bachelor minister then appointed. A smaller modern house in Knockbracken Park was purchased and the balance between the value of the houses used to form a Manse Fund against any possible future need for a larger house. Solid fuel central heating was installed in this house in 1979.

The management of a congregation is a delicate business; it must be managed effectively if it is to continue to exist but it must also be managed sensitively in sympathy with the highest ideals of its members, and a compromise between these requirements can often be difficult.   The episcopal system of church government relies on autocracy and can be very effective when the ideal autocrat can be found, but in the seventeenth century that was seldom possible.   The presbyterians rejected autocracy and pinned their faith in democracy with leaders being elected for a period and then stepping down in favour of their erstwhile subordinates. Only the session in the presbyterian system was elected for life.

Session

The Rev. William Adair (a commissioner from the Scottish General Assembly) erected a session in Belfast in July 1644. There is no record of any permanent minister being installed then, the first being the Rev. Anthony Shaw ordained in 1646. He, and indeed probably most of the congregation, was forced to flee in 1649 and the next permanent minister was the Rev. William Keyes who came in 1660 but he was later removed to Galway gaol for a short time so for considerable periods in those early years, the management of the congregation must have depended on the session.

In the first minute book of 1760 seven members are listed as forming the session and in 1768 a further 17 members were elected on the initiative of the Rev. Mackay bringing the total to 24. There is no further reference in the records to subsequent elections or to the separate activities of a session.   Apparently there was no recognised standing body of elders in 1817 as two elders were elected in that year to attend the ministers at Synod. In 1832 a resolution adopted by the committee commences with the phrase "The Committee being invested with powers to regulate the Sessional as well as the secular affairs of the congregation. . ." So although there is no record of any formal decision to dispense with a separate session it was apparently recognised as the existing situation at that date.

The Scottish regiments which came over in 1642 had ministers and sessions and it is clear from Patrick Adair's narrative that the sessions exercised strict discipline on the civilian population as well as in the regiments. Indeed the records of other presbyterian congregations show that such strict discipline was exercised by sessions at that time and much later, but it seems that the Belfast congregation rejected this new autocracy. Representative elders have been appointed from time to time either on an ad hoc or annual basis to represent the congregation at Presbytery or Synod. The first lady to be elected to this office was Miss M.E. Wood in 1957.

Although the session as a separate body appears to have withered away after the last recorded election in 1768, an attempt was apparently made in the nineteenth century to distinguish between sessional and secular business. In 1832 it was agreed that meetings of the committee be divided into two parts and that sessional affairs be considered first under the chairmanship of one of the ministers and secular business later under a lay chairman. The records indicate that this practice was followed for a few years although it is not clear on what basis the distinction was made between the two classes of business. The practice seems to have faded out as it was revived again in 1868 by a fresh resolution of the committee. Again the indications are of difficulty in establishing any clear distinction and some topics seem to have been considered indiscriminately in either part of the meeting. Raising funds was the one topic most consistently regarded as secular.

The question of creating a separate session was raised periodically over the years, notably in 1865, 1907, 1936 and 1960. The reference in the committee's report for 1864/5 reads:

"The committee have had under consideration the question of the appointment of Deacons or Elders — a time honoured custom which at one period prevailed in this as in other presbyterian houses of worship but they abstained from recommending any definite course of action until they are more fully informed as to the views of their fellow members".

Apparently their fellow members advised them to forget about it as there is no further reference to the matter at that time.

The 1907 discussion arose in connection with the draft constitution of the Non-Subscribing Presbyterian Church when the First Church urged that a session should not be obligatory but could be amalgamated with the committee, and in 1948 when a revised draft Code of Discipline was being considered they recorded the decision that "we are opposed to a session in any shape or form" in spite of the advice given to them by the Rev. Nicol Cross when he was leaving in 1937 urging the restoration of a "Session of Elders which is one of the finest and most valuable features of a living Presbyterian Church". In November 1931 the congregation adopted a written "Constitution and Rules" which provided that:

"The administration of the Spiritual Affairs of the Church including the conduct of Church Services, shall be vested in the Minister, in association with the committee".

The wording, but not the substance, of this rule was later modified and in the current version of the rules adopted in 1967 there is a paragraph headed "Session" which reads:

"The administration of the Spiritual Affairs of the Church, including the conduct of Church services, shall be vested in the Minister and Session. The Session shall be elected in the manner set forth in Rule No. 5".

Rule No. 5 deals with the election of members to the general committee so, in effect, the committee, from which members retire on a rota basis, serves as the session.

The Code of Discipline of the Non-Subscribing Presbyterian Church of Ireland (1949) provides for a session of which the minister is ex-officio moderator, but further provides "the Session shall have no jurisdiction in the temporal affairs of the congregation, and no authority over the Church Committee as such". This is obviously an attempt to define the roles and authority of two bodies which may exist in a congregation, to prevent friction between them. The First Church forestalled this possibility by making the elected committee the supreme instrument of government with powers to act as a session when necessary.

General Committee

The first minute book commences with a scheme for the support of the Old Congregation. This scheme is dated 3 February 1760 but the meeting of Heads of Families called to consider it did not convene until 3 September 1760. No explanation is given for this long delay but no doubt the fact that Carrickfergus was occupied by a French force under Thurot on 21 February 1760 and Belfast required to supply provisions for the French under threat of being razed by fire, caused a considerable diversion. Although the French forces withdrew on 26 February the air of apprehension seems to have prevailed for some months.

One of the provisions of the scheme adopted in September was:

"that a standing Committee of gentlemen, together with the Session, be appointed to regulate the affairs of the Congregation".

In spite of this resolve to have a "standing" committee it seems to have faded away since similar resolutions were adopted in 1768 and 1790. The need for a committee seems to have arisen when some particular problem such as clearing off a debt or appointing a new minister had to be dealt with. The committees, on each occasion, were appointed by meetings of Heads of Families but no indication is given how the meetings were initiated, whether by the minister, session or other individuals.

Sixteen men were elected to the 1760 committee and seven were to form "a Board (quorum) with powers to act on behalf of the congregation". They were to hold stated quarterly meetings and such others as might be necessary to deal with urgent business. The committee was to concern itself primarily with matters of finance, fixing pew rents and supervising the collection and disbursement of funds. A chairman and secretary were to be elected annually. This committee met once in 1764, twice in 1765 and once in 1766. By 1768 it was apparently considered defunct as a meeting of Heads of Families resolved that a committee be appointed to examine the accounts and manage the affairs of the congregation. This was the year in which the Rev. Thomas Drennan died.

On this occasion a committee of 45 members was elected and in addition the session was increased to 24. The committee also invited other heads of families who so desired to attend their meetings and for a time subsequently meetings were described as meetings of "Committee and other Heads of Families". No indication is given in the records of the reason for this drastic change in management from the 1760 resolve that a Board of seven would have powers to act on behalf of the congregation but one can surmise criticism of high-handed action by the former committee resulting in this attempt to involve as many members as possible in decision making. If this was the aim it was not achieved for attendance at meetings averaged about twelve over the next few years. Eventually in 1771 it was again agreed that seven members should constitite a "Board" with full powers to act on behalf of the congregation.

The business of the committee at this time was concerned mainly with the allocation of seats and collection of pew rents. There is no mention of negotiations with the Earl of Donegall for the lease obtained in 1767, the only reference to it being in 1772 when it was deposited with Mr. J.G. Smith for the perusal of members "who may incline to read it".

The sub-committee appointed in 1781 to plan and supervise the re-building of the meeting house appears to have replaced the main committee at that time and to have attended to all the business concerning the congregation. After it completed its work in 1783 there is no further record of any meetings until 1790 (the year in which Dr. Crombie died) when a meeting of Heads of Families once more resolved to elect a committee to regulate and manage the affairs of the congregation. This time they decided on a committee of seven, perhaps impressed by what had been accomplished by the small building committee ten years earlier or recognising that attendance by members of a large committee had been poor the last time they tried that. However on this occasion they decided to ensure good attendance by fixing a fine of one British shilling (to be placed in the Poor Box) for non-attendance. At the first meeting five attended and two were fined but this is the last reference to fines.

This committee was to meet four times each year, at 2 o'clock on the first Sunday of each quarter, and be replaced by a new committee elected at the beginning of each year. There is no record of whether it was re-elected each year but in 1798 two members were elected to replace two of the original seven who had died and two additional to increase the total to nine. This committee met fairly regularly for the next fourteen years under the chairmanship of Dr. Bruce.

An important advance in administration took place in 1812 (the year in which the Rev. Wm. Bruce was ordained as assistant to his father) when the regular annual meeting of the congregation was instituted. It was resolved that Heads of Families should meet annually on the first Sunday in June and this provided the opportunity to review the committee. In that year the committee was increased to eleven elected members plus four ex-officio members (two treasurers and two collectors of stipend) if not elected in the ballot. In 1819 the size of the committee was increased again by making the three members of the musical committee ex-officio members of the general committee. In 1839 it was decided to increase the number of elected members to 17 with authority to appoint from amongst themselves or other members of the congregation a committee to take charge of the choir, but in the following year the former system of electing a separate musical committee was reverted to.

The next major change in the structure of the committee was foreshadowed in the annual report for 1868 which contained the following statement:

"Hitherto there has been a General Committee of twelve whose members usually continue in office without variation excepting on death or resignation. With a view to excite a more extended interest in our Congregational affairs this Committee have come to the conclusion of recommending that four persons appointed on the General Committee at the annual meeting shall retire at the end of each year and shall not be eligible for re-election for the ensuing year".

This principle was adopted and it was agreed that three members be elected each year to serve a four-year period and then be ineligible for re-election for one year. This device for rotating committee membership around the congregation was only partially successful as an examination of the records over the years shows that a high proportion of those so retired was re-elected after the lapse of one year. However, the rate of change of personnel every fifth year between 1880 and 1975 was about 40% compared with about half that rate previously due to death and resignation.

This basic structure for the general committee adopted in 1869 has remained until the present time. In 1893 the number of elected members was increased to 16 i.e. four people for a four-year period but in 1963 it was again reduced to 12 mainly because of the increase in the number of ex-officio members. The 1760 committee was to be a committee of "gentlemen" and it remained an all male body until 1928 when Mrs. Hume and Miss Armstrong were the first ladies elected to it. The number of ladies elected has increased since then but is still not quite half of the membership. In 1979 Mrs. S. Stewart was elected vice-chairman and was the first lady elected to this office.

The chairmanship of the committee has caused some agitation from time to time over the years. In the presbyterian system the minister is traditionally moderator of session but not necessarily chairman of the committee. In 1783 the Rev. Crombie was appointed secretary to the committee for a brief period so it must then have had a lay chairman. On the other hand the Rev. Dr. Bruce almost invariably presided over committee meetings during his ministry. The record gives no hint that the division of committee business into sessional and secular in the last century arose out of any disagreement about chairmanship of the committee but it may well have been one of the considerations that led to that peculiar arrangement.

The question of chairmanship of committee arose during the ministry of the Rev. Nicol Cross. Although he came to the church in 1928 he was not elected chairman of the committee until 1932. After Mr. Rossington resigned Mr. R.M. Laird had given notice to move in committee that in future a lay chairman preside at committee and while no formal decision is recorded his proposal was obviously kept in mind for some years. During this period there had been correspondence in the Non-Subscribing Magazine about the chairmanship of church committees mainly advocating that the minister should be chairman as a matter of right. Mr. Cross was re-elected annually from 1932 but in 1937 he refused to accept nomination on the ground that the minister was automatically chairman and therefore no election should take place. However the committee still elected him but, as he declined to accept, the vice-chairman presided at meetings and the committee decided to refer the matter to Synod.

A few months later the committee received a communication from the Presbytery of Antrim to whom Synod had referred the matter. The substance of their reply was that while the Constitution of the Non-Subscribing Church did not specifically provide that the minister should be chairman of the committee (in order to accommodate constituent congregations which did not have a presbyterian tradition) Presbytery felt that it was desirable that the minister should preside over the governing body in a congregation and commended this arrangement to the committee. A proposal to elect Mr. Cross was withdrawn to await his opinion on the matter and at the next meeting a letter from him said that while he considered it not unreasonable for the committee to adhere to its printed rules, he felt it unwise for a minister to be competing with others for the chairmanship and as a result possibly become the nominee of a faction within the congregation. Such a development would inevitably tend to undermine his position as minister. He therefore considered it in the best interests of the congregation to decline nomination. In his letter of resignation in March 1938 the Rev. Cross used the phrase "freed from the frustrations which I feel have lately hampered my ministry in the First Church . . . ." but whether chairmanship of the committee was one of them is left to be deduced. Referring to his successor the Rev. Cross wrote "Choose the right man and once chosen . . . give him the authority and following his office and responsibility deserve" and that advice rings an echo of the chairmanship problem.

It is obviously a difficult problem. Committee members will wish to have the minister's views on matters before them and ministers will often have quite definite views, but to present these from the chair and at the same time preserve the atmosphere of impartial chairmanship requires considerable skill and tact. Church committees are vulnerable to a feeling of being hustled; members come to a meeting from widely varying backgrounds having had their minds focussed on a variety of quite different problems. They need time to re-focus on the problems of a congregation and for consideration of the implications of different courses of action before being pressed to reach a decision. The minister by reason of his calling and background is likely to reach a decision much more quickly but needs to be able to exercise patience while members adjust themselves to fresh lines of thought.

The frequency of committee meetings has varied from quarterly to monthly over the centuries. In the late eighteenth and early nineteenth-centuries quarterly meetings were the rule. For example in 1790 it was decided that the quarterly meeting of the committee would be held at 2 p.m. on the first Sunday of each quarter. The 1815 annual meeting directed that the committee should meet after the second service on the first Sunday of each month without further summons though in 1817 the committee ordered that hereafter a card shall be hung in the porch intimating the dates on which the committee. meets. Attendance at this period usually varied around 4 to 6 members i.e. about 30%.

In 1838 the committee decided to meet immediately after the morning service each month but the frequency changed either by accident or design during the period of the missing minute book and in 1870 it was decided "to hold monthly meetings instead of quarterly as formerly". However in 1877 the meetings were again being referred to as quarterly but in 1884 it was agreed that meetings should be bi-monthly on Sundays. In 1921 it was agreed to hold regular monthly meetings on the first Sunday of each month, but in 1923 this was changed to the first Friday and has remained so since. It is interesting that in the eighteenth century meetings were generally held on week days while in the nineteenth century, when the population of Belfast moved away from the city centre, Sunday meetings became popular. Then in the twentieth century, when means of transport improved, week day meetings were again adopted.

There are few references to the length of meetings; on one occasion in 1901 a meeting was adjourned after two hours and unfinished business held over to the next meeting. Apparently it was considered that meetings should be over within two hours.

On another occasion in 1907 business was postponed because "the hour was late". It seems as if unusual measures were taken at this time to curtail the length of meetings, for in October 1906 a special meeting was held to confirm the minutes of all meetings since the previous January. These occupied 71 pages of the minute book and so must have taken a considerable time to read. Six members attended that meeting.

The quorum fixed for the 1760 committee was seven and the quorum in the current rules two centuries later is also seven, but that number must have been difficult to achieve in the nineteenth century for in 1863 the quorum was reduced to three. Indeed at some meetings about that time it seems as if only the secretary and treasurer were present, although reports were presented and minutes recorded as if for a full meeting. Attendance at committees has always been high in recent years. This was perhaps ensured by a resolution passed at the annual meeting in 1927 that the ballot for committee members be confined to those present at the meeting. This was later modified to include any whom the proposer could testify to be willing to act if elected.

A church committee, like all governing bodies, tends to become the focus for blame for all the ills of the community over which it governs. However, over the centuries the committee of the First Church has shown commendable collective wisdom and statesmanship. A number of major building projects were undertaken in circumstances of considerable difficulty but were eventually brought to a successful conclusion. Problems with ministers were also handled with considerable skill, the main examples of these being with the Rev. J. Kirk Pike and the Rev. D. Walmsley.

The Rev. Pike was called as successor to the Rev. A. Gordon on 22 June 1890 and was installed the following September in a celebration ending with a conversazione in the Exhibition Hall in Botanic Gardens. His call was initially for three years; no reason is recorded for this unusual arrangement and no doubt it would have extended indefinitely had everything gone smoothly The only suggestion of tension between Mr. Pike and the committee was when his third application for a £75 advance of salary in 1893 was reduced to £50 (£75 had been advanced in previous years) the committee "deprecating these applications". However on 9 April 1893 the committee had before it a document signed by 43 seat holders and 28 worshippers requesting consideration of Mr. Pike's position now that the three years were coming to an end and referring to an absence of spiritual and intellectual power and want of stimulating and helpful influence over the young and a great want of active energy. This document was passed to Mr. Pike who handed in his resignation on 30 April "to prevent an unhappy division" and requesting one year's stipend as compensation. The committee resolved to accept his resignation and to raise a donation of £300 by voluntary subscription. A congregational meeting called for 9 May was adjourned to the 14th because of poor attendance. At the adjourned meeting a number of resolutions and amendments were proposed and debated but eventually the committee's recommendation was accepted and an appeal issued for subscriptions to the donation.

On 6 August a deputation from a section of the congregation met the committee to request the retention of Mr. Pike stating that a majority of the congregation now favoured this course. This placed the committee in a difficult position as Mr. Pike's resignation had been accepted and the collection for his presentation was in progress. However they did not blankly refuse further consideration, as they might have done, but asked the deputation to obtain signatures to substantiate their claim. When produced, the list contained 82 signatures out of a possible total of 196. The committee now decided to ask this faction to appoint three representatives to meet three appointed by the original petitioners against Mr. Pike's retention with the committee "to ascertain if there be any course that could be adopted on which the congregation could take united action". But the original petitioners declined to appoint representatives for a meeting which they thought could serve no useful purpose since Mr. Pike's resignation had been accepted unanimously at a large meeting of the congregation when both points of view had been debated in a friendly spirit. The committee then agreed to take no further action unless a formal requisition for a meeting was submitted, which was duly done by Mr. Pike's supporters.

As Mr. Pike's resignation took effect in September an approach was made to the Northern Presbytery of Antrim about supplies during the vacancy. The Presbytery appointed Mr. Pike constant supply and recommended the committee to call the congregational meeting as requisitioned, thus satisfying a requirement of the code that no matter could be placed before a congregation contrary to the decision of the committee unless with the sanction of Presbytery. The secretary asked for a copy of the code and on perceiving that it was the code of the Remonstrant Synod pointed out that the Northern Presbytery of Antrim did not belong to this Synod, to which Presbytery, rather lamely, replied that this was an old established rule of presbyterianism. To this the committee replied that they considered it unwise to have Mr. Pike as supply as:

"any such appointment would be an insuperable obstacle to the hearing of other ministers and be at variance with the apparent intention and purpose of the congregation in accepting Mr. Pike's resignation and agreeing to pay him a sum of not less than £300"; but they did agree to call the congregational meeting.

For this meeting a special report was printed and issued to members summarising and explaining the events necessitating the meeting:

"The committee, moving strictly on the lines of well established precedents, had already made some enquiries about a suitable locum-tenens to fill our pulpit, preliminary to the more important steps necessary to enable the Congregation to decide on the choice of a permanent minister, when their proceedings were arrested by the intervention of certain members of the Congregation, who on second thoughts had organised an important movement, with the avowed object of inducing the Congregation to retrace its steps and agree to the reinstatement of Mr. Pike as our Minister. . . . .".

"The proposal formulated at that particular juncture, and backed, as was alleged, by a majority of the Congregation, made it plain to the Committee that it would not be possible for them to take in hand and carry to a satisfactory issue the negotiations and arrangements, which it had been customary for the Committee to undertake on the occasion of a vacancy in our pulpit, unless and until clothed with new authority by a vote of the Congregation . . . .

It only remains for the Committee to make an earnest appeal to their fellow members of the Congregation to approach the consideration of the question to be submitted to them in a dispassionate and conciliatory spirit, and with a single eye to the best and highest interests of the Congregation, which should be paramount in our minds to every personal interest."

The special congregational meeting was held on 22 October and was well attended. The first business was to agree a Poll list which included the names of members eligible to vote and the amount of their contributions in the previous year. A proposal that Presbytery be asked to appoint Mr. Pike locum tenens for a year was lost to an amendment to proceed with the appointment of a new minister by a Synodical majority (i.e. two thirds of the members subscribing at least two thirds of the stipend). The result recorded was 90 votes representing £196.0.9 for the amendment against 38 votes representing £98.18.0. Clearly a deep division along this line would have crippled the congregation and it must have been a great relief to the committee that the amendment was carried unanimously when put to the meeting as a substantive motion. No doubt some members of committee favoured the minority view but it is clear that the committee as a body concentrated on ascertaining the majority view and then persuading the minority to accept that view which they did with success. Incidentally Mr. Pike apparently came to share the view that he was not cut out for ministerial work as he subsequently became Professor of English Literature in Tokyo University in Japan.

In the following year the congregation decided to call the Rev. Douglas Walmsley, it being stated in the course of correspondence with him that the appointment was for life subject only to "removal by Synodical majority". It was also decided to delay his installation until the Northern Presbytery of Antrim joined the Remonstrant Synod. The committee then set about urging the Northern Presbytery to reunite with the Presbytery of Antrim and seek admission to the Remonstrant Synod:

"so as to have a real and proper form of Presbyterianism instead of the mongrel description we have at present . . . under which no one can define their position nor tell what rules they are guided by".

There was considerable opposition to be overcome in Presbytery but eventually the Presbyteries reunited in September 1894 and the Rev. Douglas Walmsley was installed on 23 January 1895.

A special meeting of the committee was held on 17 December 1905 in response to a requisition signed by 17 lady members of the congregation. In the course of their memorial the ladies said

"We find that our Church does not now hold the position in the City which it was our pride and pleasure to see it occupy in times which we love to remember and which are not long past. It is not represented as it should be at the Public Meetings which are held for Charities and other objects, nor on the Boards and Charitable Committees of the City. It is not for us, gentlemen, to discover the cause, or suggest a remedy, for this state of things; we look to you as the appointed guardians of the interests and welfare of our Church to endeavour to do so".

Mr. Walmsley, who presided at this meeting read a letter he had written in reply to the memorial. After dealing with a number of points made he wrote:

"If I am now to be told that my teaching is no longer approved, my work no longer satisfies or my manner of life is challenged . . . . . . then I ask to know in what I have offended. . . I am ready to resign".

He then withdrew from the meeting "to leave you to speak of these matters unembarrassed by my presence".

A letter from Mr. H.W. McFadden then presented, listed a number of complaints viz;-

1. The young people were not coming to Church after Sunday School because the Minister takes insufficient interest in them.
2. No preparatory class for Communion was held because Mr. Walmsley considered it unnecessary.
3. There were delays in visiting the elderly sick.

The committee after some discussion adopted a resolution expressing their utmost confidence in the minister and appointed a sub-committee to draft a detailed statement containing the view of the committee. It met again a few days later and adopted the statement which commended a number of matters to the minister's attention and ended "the committee hope their suggestions will be accepted in the same friendly spirit in which they are made and that all can work together in harmony". Both the ladies and the minister accepted the committee's suggestions as a basis for fruitful work but within a month the minister resigned. On being pressed by the committee to reconsider his resignation he wrote "an insult has been passed upon me which I cannot overlook". At the congregational meeting to consider the minister's resignation the committee again concentrated on the need to maintain congregational unity and this was achieved.

Both these incidents contained the seeds of serious fragmentation of the congregation, averted by the diplomatic and sensitive manner in which the committee acted, and there were many other occasions when committee members were required to ignore their individual preference for the good of the whole which is the hallmark of statesmanship and the essence of democracy. The committee usually met in the session room of the church or in a room in the central hall. An occasional meeting was held in the manse and amongst the venues mentioned for rare meetings outside church premises were the Old Sugar House and the Board Room of the Ulster Bank.

Music Committee

This committee, known until 1845 as the musical committee, also had somewhat ad hoc origins. The first reference to it is in a resolution passed by the general committee in November 1814 "that the late musical committee are requested to take the necessary steps for securing a second voice". In 1808 the congregation had resolved "that the committee be invested with powers for the improvement of the Psalmody" so possibly it had appointed a sub-committee for this purpose though there is no record of such an appointment.

In May 1816 it was resolved that the members of the committee for improving the Psalmody be Mr. Houston, Henry Joy, Saml. S. Thomson and Saml. Smith with powers to call in such other persons as may be able to assist. At the annual meeting in June 1816 it is recorded that Dr. Thomson reported on behalf of the musical committee and in the following year three people, Dr. Thomson and Messrs Joy and Houston were appointed to the musical committee "to continue with the same powers and funds" though these are not previously recorded. In 1819 the three members of the musical committee were made ex-officio members of the general committee and at the same annual meeting two directions were given in relation to music; one to the general committee to determine whether a teacher of the choir ought to be permanently continued, and the other to the musical committee to see that the music was so regulated as to suit the voices of the congregation. This apparently made the distinction between the roles of the general committee in controlling expenditure and of the musical committee for the technicalities of the music. Mr. F. Whitla was added to the musical committee in 1824, and in 1828 it was further strengthened by the addition of Capt. Munster and Chas. Creek.

The practice of electing a separate musical committee at the annual meeting continued until 1839 when it was decided to elect a general committee of 17 with powers to appoint from among themselves or other members of the congregation a sub-committee to supervise the choir. This procedure was apparently devised to deal with a problem concerning two members of the choir — Benjamin Mitchell and Mary Hughes. Mary seems to have been a daughter of William Hughes, former clerk, whose release from the army had been purchased in 1808. In 1827 it was agreed to give 5 guineas to the widow of Wm. Hughes and to offer Margt. Hughes 2 guineas for her past services in the choir (the names Margt. and Mary are used on different occasions but appear to refer to the same person). In May 1838 the Rev. Bruce reported to the committee that as a result of enquiries made by Mr. Porter and himself, they were of the opinion "that Mary Hughes should be prevented from attending in the choir". It was resolved to advise Mary Hughes that the committee had no further occasion for her services and to direct the musical committee to fill the vacancy. At the June meeting of the general committee the musical committee reported "that they were not yet prepared to report upon the measures proper to be adopted for filling the vacancy" and at the August meeting it was noted that there was no report from the musical committee.

There is no further reference to this matter until April 1839 when Miss Smith applied to the committee for leave to bring back Margt. Hughes to assist in the choir, "who had been removed some time ago for levity of conduct". In this minute "irregular" had been crossed out and "levity of" written in. At the annual meeting a few weeks later the first item of business considered was to alter the method of electing the musical committee as described above. The matter was obviously causing considerable agitation as there were many other items of important business to come before this meeting and the actual election of the committee came much later in the agenda.

At its next meeting the general committee appointed a sub-committee of five ladies and seven men to superintend the choir (this was the first time ladies had been elected to any committee). At the September meeting of the general committee the case of Benjamin Mitchell and Mary Hughes was referred to the musical committee. This committee met in October when apparently only three members attended — Dr. Thomson, Marcus Ward and the secretary — in spite of the large sub-committee appointed in May. The minute of their meeting reads: "The cases of Benjamin Mitchell and Mary Hughes was considered but the committee declined to decide upon them on the grounds that the matter did not come properly under their cognizance having reference only to their immorality". Clearly the musical committee considered the quality of the music to be their first priority, but their stand was in vain for both were dismissed from the choir at the next meeting of the general committee. However in view of Mr. Mitchell's long membership of the choir the treasurer was instructed to pay him an additional six weeks salary. There is no record of when Mitchell joined but there is a reference to his membership of the choir in 1821. This method of putting "backbone" into the musical committee having failed, the former practice of electing it at the annual meeting was reverted to in the following year, 1840, when 12 members including four ladies were elected to it. Apparently this practice continued though the missing book leaves a gap in the record at this time.

At the annual meeting in 1862 it was decided to elect 15 members to the music committee. No reason is given for the increase but it did not last for in the following year the number was reduced to five "the present number being found inconveniently large for the proper transaction of business". The number of members of this committee varied over the next three decades until 1896 when it was fixed at eight. It had again become an all male body. In 1885 the general committee decided that five ladies be invited to sit with the music committee as an experiment with a view to their being elected members. At the annual meeting in 1887 it was resolved "that it be a suggestion to the Music Committee to consider the propriety of including ladies amongst those to be proposed next year for election on that Committee". Apparently the suggestion was accepted as Miss McTear and Miss Bruce were elected in 1888. During the interregnum of ministry in 1906 Miss Bruce frequently presided over the music committee so the experiment must have been considered successful. When the size of this committee was fixed at eight in 1896 it was placed on the same type of rota basis as had been applied to the general committee i.e. two members were elected each year to serve a four-year period and were then ineligible for re-election for one year. In 1906 the number was increased to 12 (three elected each year for a four-year period) but in 1936 was reduced to six (two each year for a three-year period) and has remained so since.

It seems anomalous that the music committee should be elected at the annual meeting when other important sub-committees are elected by the general committee. In matters of expenditure and appointments the music committee acts as a sub-committee making recommendations to the general committee but it does assume direct responsibility for the type and quality of the music and should, therefore, draw upon the best expertise available within the whole congregation. In spite of this peculiar constitutional arrangement there have been very few instances of friction between the music committee and the general committee.

In 1891 the music committee was concerned about the lack of support for the music fund and proposed an additional levy on pew rents for music but this was rejected by the annual meeting. In 1911 the music committee made recommendations about alterations for choir seating and the property sub-committee complained that the music committee was acting "ultra vires" as it had no powers to spend church funds. However this matter was settled amicably. In 1919 a member of the general committee proposed that it take over the work of the music committee as he did not approve their method of conducting their business but his proposal found no support. The music committee decided in 1934 to take no action on a request from the general committee to secure an improvement in the music. Apart from these minor ruffles the organisation appears to have operated very smoothly over the years.

Sub-Committees

At the end of the eighteenth and during the nineteenth centuries the committee appointed ad hoc sub-committees for specific projects either to examine and report on some matter or to undertake some specific task. One of the earliest and perhaps the most notable of these was the building committee appointed in 1781 to plan and supervise the re-building of the meeting house. Repairs and redecoration were often entrusted to sub-committees such as the one appointed in 1835 to arrange the installation of gas lighting. In 1836 a sub-committee was established to look after the property and given powers to order repairs without reference to the general committee and reference is made to such a committee from time to time over the years though no formal arrangements existed for its appointment or re-appointment until 1924. Similarly finance sub-committees were appointed from time to time, usually when there was a need to increase funds.

The first reference to a pews committee was in 1908 when one was appointed to locate seats for a list of applicants. This committee arranged for the construction of pews in the space in the gallery vacated when the organ and choir were brought to ground level. It remained in existence and met from time to time although no formal means of re-appointment was provided until 1924. This committee dealt with allocation of pews and occasionally considered the problem of arrears of stipend — matters which formed the main business of the general committee in the first century of its existence. In 1894 a "strangers committee" had been appointed with the role of attending to visitors and making them feel welcome but it faded out although the problem of welcoming visitors remained and was referred to in the general committee from time to time.

Prior to 1890 reference was made occasionally to a library committee but there is no record of its origin. However in that year it was decided to appoint a library committee of four, one member being elected each year to serve a four-year stint and then being ineligible for re-election for one year. After 1928 two librarians were elected each year with no further reference to a committee. In 1924 it was agreed that the general committee should have standing sub-committees for finance, property and pews which are appointed annually ever since. The pews committee was re-named membership committee in 1960. A Central Hall management committee was first appointed in 1918 and placed on a permanent basis in 1926. It was revived in 1959 when the new hall was built.

Over the years a succession of individuals have taken an interest in the church property and were often asked by the committee to plan or supervise alterations or repairs. Because of the unofficial nature of their status it is not possible to produce a definitive list of such people but the following would have had a place in such a list: J. Galt Smith, T. Ritchie, E.J. Harland, W.T. Hamilton, Jas. Davidson, T.H. McMurray, A. Hunter, R.B. McCutcheon, Wm. McRobert and F. Smyth. In 1956 the need for some one individual to supervise property and place before the committee matters requiring attention was recognised by the creation of an office of property steward. Mr. J. Meneely was the first property steward and was succeeded by Wm. McMurray, Fred McMurray, Ian McMurray, Ralph Trueick and Jimmy Hynds.

Other Organisations

This seems the appropriate place to mention other organisations referred to in the records which were involved in congregational acivities. About twenty such bodies are mentioned incidentally but there are few specific records of their organisation and management. In earlier years such organisations tended to be mainly charitable bodies but in more recent times aimed at providing recreational and social activities for members. A few have had the more serious objectives of extending thought and knowledge. A Ladies' Clothing Society existed in the eighteenth and nineteenth centuries, but the only references are to collections taken in support of its work. Presumably it was the forerunner of the Ladies' Sewing Society mentioned towards the end of the nineteenth century as making and distributing clothes among the poor.

The Institute of Faith and Science was formed in 1878 with the object of "cultivating Christian Faith in the light of knowledge and charity and for the promotion of Scientific and Literary tastes in a religious and Christian spirit". This interest was possibly stimulated by the meetings of the British Association for the Advancement of Science in Belfast in 1874 at which Tyndall deplored the retarding effect of religious ideas on the progress of scientific thought. The attitude of members was to integrate new knowledge into a credible religious faith. In 1901 the Institute recommended the congregation to appoint a Social Evenings Committee to take over its functions so by that time it had become a mainly social body.

In October 1881 the committee accepted a proposal from some ladies in the congregation to form a Ladies Committee to supervise the church and hall and advise generally on decoration and maintenance. Presumably the ladies were unhappy with the results of the efforts of the all-male committee. This committee consisted of four ladies at first but was increased to eight in 1896 (two being elected each year for a four-year period) and continued thus until 1927 when it was disbanded a few years after the formation of a branch of the Womens League. There are no minutes for meetings of the Ladies Committee but references to them in other reports suggest that they played a leading part in the congregation's charitable activities especially during the First World War. A Band of Hope was initiated in 1884 and the last reference to its meetings in the annual report for 1915 records an average attendance of about 70 at four meetings held during that year.

A Sunday School Dorcas Society is first mentioned in the report for 1889. This society seems to have met monthly or fortnightly to make garments which were sold at half the cost of the material used, at an Annual Sale, when a number of "poor women" were entertained to tea. The last reference to a sale was in 1917 and the last reference to the Society was in Miss Laird's obituary notice in 1921. A proposal was circulated among members in 1895 for the formation of a Unitarian Club and in 1896 a resolution of thanks for the use of the Central Hall by the Club was received. A Literary Guild is mentioned in the report for 1897 as having been formed the previous year. It had an average attendance of 28 at meetings which took the form of readings by members. In the report for 1922 reference is made to a First Church Fellowship for young people. It apparently met monthly but there is no indication as to how long it survived.

The 1923 report records the formation during the past twelve months of a branch of the British League of Unitarian and other Liberal Christian Women which met fortnightly in the afternoons during the autumn and winter. The church calendar for March 1930 contains a report on the first performance by the Rosemary Dramatic Club when the Central Hall was filled to overflowing. In October 1934 a deputation of young people proposed the establishment of a Billiards Club but the committee declined to give their assent. A year later a club, known as the Rosemary Club, was formed and when it was presented with a billiard table some time later the committee agreed to its acceptance. This seems like a manoeuvre on the part of the young people to circumvent the scruples of their elders. Unfortunately committee's first reaction proved right as they were obliged to withdraw permission for the club to use the hall following complaints from the caretaker, other tenants and the police in 1937. The formation of a Discussion Circle in 1937 is described in the report for that year as "a development full of interest and promise".

In October 1938 the committee expressed approval and appreciation of a proposal by Miss M.E. Wood to form a junior branch of the Womens League to meet in the evenings intended for women whose work prevented them from attending the afternoon meetings of the senior branch. The branches were amalgamated in 1955 and continue to play a vital role in the life of the congregation.

A Men's Circle was formed in 1946 to meet for recreational acivity on Wednesday evenings. It existed for a number of years under a variety of titles. The opening of the new Central Hall in 1959 saw the revival of the Dramatic Society and Men's Club and the formation of a Youth Guild and a Badminton Club. However the civil distrubances of the 1970's severely limited congregational evening activities.

The rise and decline of these various organisations in the congregation over the centuries reflects the evolution of society in general. Those organisations which had charitable objectives were overtaken by the development of state social services while those aimed at educational and cultural progress were absorbed in more widely based community movements. Members of the congregation were much involved in such wider developments in the general community. The annual series of Central Hall lectures arranged during the 1960s on religious and social topics were brought to an end by the civil disturbances but it had been noted that attendance at them consisted mainly of members who felt an obligation to support them. This kind of activity by local organisations had been supplanted by the mass media which provide a wide variety of professional, well informed discussion and comment in the home. The activity of the congregation has tended to become confined to its original role of providing a venue for worship and assisting individuals to form a satisfying philosophy of life.

The Constituency

Decisions of the congregation were made by "seat holders" in the eighteenth and nineteenth centuries gradually passing into the hands of "members" by the twentieth century. "Seat holders" were usually heads of families who paid a pew rent for the whole family by taking the requisite number of sittings in a pew, while "members" were individuals who contributed to congregational funds. There is no record of any formal rules relating to eligibility to vote at congregational meetings prior to 1869 but in the annual report for that year, considered at the annual meeting in May 1870, the following paragraph was included:

"In making up a Poll List for the Election of a Minister, it has always been the law and practice of this Congregation, and of the ecclesiastical body with which it is connected, to require the concurrence of two-thirds of the persons voting, paying in the aggregate two-thirds of the amount of stipend contributed by those voting to make an election . . . It is also necessary that in order to have a vote, the seatholder must have been such for at least six months prior to the occurrence of the vacancy to be filled up, and not to be in arrear".

At the next annual meeting in May 1871 a list of nine "Regulations for the exercise of the congregational franchise in the First Presbyterian Church, Belfast" were presented and adopted. These included:

I. The Constituency of this Congregation consists of adult persons ordinarily joining in its religious worship, contributing steadily to its support, and duly registered in its Records for a period of not less than twelve months.

V. A Contributor whose stipend remains unpaid for twelve months, and who omits to pay his arrear within three months after being applied to for the same in writing, will be held to have relinquished his connexion with the Congregation.

IX. For the decision of any other question (i.e. other than the appointment of a minister) that may be brought before the Congregation, a simple majority of the duly registered electors, present and voting, and contributing at least one half of the Annual Stipend paid by all the electors present and voting is sufficient.

Regulations for the letting of pews and sittings were adopted in 1873 (with amendments in 1886, 1891, and 1901) and included each year in the annual report until 1914. These were:

1. That lettings of Pews or Sittings by the Collector of Stipend be provisional, subject to confirmation by the Congregational Committee.

2. That as regards new applicants, the distinction between first and second class pews on the ground floor be abolished; and that all sittings be charged at a uniform rent of £1 per annum; or for the pews recently altered or erected in the neighbourhood of the pulpit, £5 per annum for the entire pew.

3. That applicants wishing for an entire pew have priority over those who only apply for part of a pew.

4. That when a sitting is let to a newcomer in a pew already partly occupied, notice of the proposed new letting shall be given to the existing occupants, prior to the confirmation of the new letting by the Committee.

5. That persons who were formerly seatholders, but who had removed from Belfast, shall, on return, be permitted to resume the pews which they had originally occupied, if still available.

6. That other applicants be permitted to select accommodation in vacant or available pews, choosing in the order of the dates of their respective application.

7. That any member desiring to vacate a pew or sitting must give six months notice in writing, to the Collector of Stipend, or general committee, previous to one of the half-yearly gales. And on the death of a member, when the pew or sitting is not retained by his representative, his executors or administrators will be liable for the current half-yearly gale and arrears, if any.

It is perhaps significant that these rather legalistic regulations were adopted at a time when the church secretary was a solicitor but it is typical of the tendency in all organisations, including states, to add detailed amendments to legislation and regulation as problems arise with definition thus, in time, accumulating a mass of detailed rules which threaten to smother the original objectives of the organisation. Frequent pruning back to the original rootstock is necessary to maintain fresh growth. In 1931 the congregation adopted a formal "Constitution and Rules" embodying general principles and discarding the detailed regulations which had accumulated over the years.

The concept of pew rents became obsolete when the congregation adopted a system of "Freewill Offerings" in 1930 and was finally laid to rest in 1962 when it was decided that individual members would be no longer associated with particular pews. The last reference in the records to pew rents was in 1922 when it was decided to simplify existing rates by specifying a rate of £1 for seats on the ground floor and fifteen shillings for seats in the gallery. However these changes left unresolved the problem of defining controlling membership. The question was debated in 1967 during a discussion on the revision of the constitution and rules. The existing rules provided for a minimum subscription of thirteen shillings per year as the qualification for controlling membership. It was argued that such a provision was unchristian, that church membership should be open to anyone who wished to attend, irrespective of whether or not they wished to contribute towards its funds. On the other hand it was contended that controlling membership should not be extended to those unwilling to support it financially and who might adopt an irresponsible attitude to the facilities provided by others. The problem was shelved at that stage by leaving the minimum figure unchanged even though, with inflation, it had become unrealistic; but it is a problem which is likely to call for resolution at some future date, perhaps by providing for both controlling and other membership.

There is little information about membership in the seventeenth and eighteenth centuries. In the earliest records for the second half of the eighteenth century names occur only in pew allocations or committee membership and inconsistencies in spelling reduce the value of these. Gordon (11) gives a list of stipend payers in 1775 and a list of members, with some addresses, for 1790 said to be derived from Dr. Bruce's manuscripts. These have been included in the appendix of this volume along with lists at quarter-century intervals since, that is about a generation.

The first printed list known to exist in the records is for the year 1812 (when it was decided to hold annual meetings of the congregation) and there are lists for almost all years since then. Some lists for the second and third decades of the nineteenth century are pasted into minute book No. 2, and for the next forty years those available are in the scrapbook. Lists are given in annual reports since 1868 and addresses of members have been included since 1889. The early lists are names of heads of families and therefore not complete lists of members but in recent years the roll of constituents is essentially a complete list of members.

It can be assumed that in the seventeenth and eighteenth centuries almost all members lived within walking distance of the church and even at the end of the nineteenth century a large proportion lived within a radius of two or three miles. This has changed radically in the twentieth century when very few members live in the immediate neighbourhood, being mostly scattered in the suburbs and in the region around Belfast.

The congregation is small by Belfast standards and also has a greater turn-over of membership than most neighbourhood churches would experience. Some indication of this turn-over can be gleaned from the following table in which is given the number of new members who joined in a particular year and the number of those still members after intervals of five and ten years. These are crude figures in that the method of obtaining them was to note the pew number of the new member and check whether her or his name was still opposite the same pew number five and ten years hence. This method missed a) those whose names were allocated to a different pew in subsequent years, b) single ladies who changed their names on marriage, and c) those who died within the period. Examples of each of these have been observed, but a laborious examination of the lists had not been made to correct these errors since the crude figures illustrate the general trend.

Year	Number who joined that year	Number of those still members after	
		5 years	10 years
1915	12	8	4
1920	18	5	2
1925	25	14	12
1930	35	21	16
1,935	19	10	4
1940	22	15	11
1945	11	6	3
1950	17	14	9
1955	13	9	7
1960	14	12	8
1965	8	6	4
Mean	18	11	7

It has not been possible to distinguish between those who left because the church did not satisfy them and those who left for other reasons such as removal from Belfast.

It would be impossible to identify or categorise all the motives which led people to join the First Church but one of the main reasons was their inability to accept the theology of orthodox or evangelical bodies and their desire for a more honest stance. It has been noticed that the number of new members increased more rapidly if the church was the subject of an attack by some other body. An extract from the 1922 annual report reads:

"From October the evening attendances were perhaps the best in the history of the Church, the average on six successive Sundays being nearly 600. Perhaps the chief cause of this was the interest in, and sympathy for, our faith created by the coarse and uncalled for attacks made upon us by a notorious missionary. These attacks are no new thing. What was new and surprising was the fact that they were made from the pulpit of our nearest neighbour, the Third Presbyterian Church, Rosemary Street. Made public in the Press they created the desire on the part of many people to hear what our faith really was".

One of the recurring problems for the committee was to devise effective and acceptable means of making the principles and ideals of the congregation known to those likely to be in sympathy with them. Frequently, new members expressed their delight at finding a church which so closely met their standards of what a church ought to be but who had discovered it through some chance encounter and urged the need to make its existence known to others of like mind. The congregation had always set its face against proselytism; it has never claimed to possess the only truth or that other faiths were devoid of truth. This attitude severely limits the acceptable ways in which it can make its principles known so that people can choose to join or not as they judge proper for themselves. It also creates problems in dealing with visitors to the church; the desire to avoid giving any impression of pressing membership on anyone often gave rise to the complaint that visitors were ignored and allowed to feel unwelcome. It also gave rise to the problem of the loss of young people from the congregation over the years frequently referred to as drifting away after leaving Sunday school. This was a difficult problem for a church that emphasised the right, indeed the duty, of individuals to ponder the issues of life and study how these were catered for by other denominations and then make their choice of what seemed best for them.

Finance

The earlier committees were primarily concerned with fixing pew rents and allocating seats to members. Thus one of the first resolutions of the 1760 committee was "that the seats should be numbered and rated in the most equal manner so as to raise the annual sum required for the minister and clerk and a surplus for contingences".
The rates fixed by that committee were:—

19 double seats below at 6s. 6d. per month	£6.3.6
4 double square seats below at 5s. 5d. per month	1.1.8
24 single seats below at 3s. 3d. per month	3.18.0
21 double seats above at 3s. 3d. per month	3.8.3
20 single seats above at 1s. 7½d per month	1.12.6
	16.3.11

The term "seats" used here appears to have been synonymous with pews as the total seating capacity of the old house was reckoned at 723 in 1781. If all the seats had been occupied these rates would have yielded £194.7.0 per year, but this apparently did not produce much surplus over current costs as an appeal was made at the same time for additional voluntary subscriptions to pay off the debt due to Mr. Mackay. When some repairs were needed in 1765 it was agreed to collect an additional month's stipend, and again in 1775 it was agreed to collect three months' stipend to repay money due to the treasurer.

The financial burden on members was alleviated in subsequent years partly by ministers becoming involved in teaching work and partly by Regium Donum. Dr. Crombie established the Belfast Academy in 1785, and Dr. Bruce continued it when he was called to the First Church in 1790 until he retired from the Academy in 1822. The Rev. Wm. Bruce held the Professorship in Latin, Greek and Hebrew in the Academical Institution from 1821 till 1849. Apparently the congregation was unhappy about these teaching appointments, for when the Rev. J. Scott Porter was called in 1832 the committee expressed the wish that he would not take up any other work except in advancement of his academic status. No doubt the exception applied to his appointment as Professor of Divinity in the Institution from 1840-1850.

In his letter to the committee in August 1869 in which the Rev. Scott Porter offered to commute his Regium Donum for the benefit of the congregation under the Irish Church Act he stated that having been ordained prior to 1839 his Regium Donum was £92. 6. 2 per annum (the maximum rate for ministers ordained after that date was £70). At this time the salary paid to the minister by the congregation was £240 per annum so Regium Donum was a significant supplement. A sub-committee consisting of Thomas L'Estrange, William Hartley and E.J. Harland appointed to consider the effect of the loss of Regium Donum on congregational finances produced a seating plan of the church with a recommendation for five different rates of pew rents ranging from £1 to 2/6d. per sitting so as to provide sufficient income to maintain salaries at the existing level. The termination of Regium Donum also stimulated an interest in the income from property as the lease of the old manse premises was coming to an end.

The following crude totals under the various headings in the church account over the past century indicate the main sources of income and expenditure.

Year	INCOME				EXPENDITURE			
	Stipend	Music	General Purposes	Rents	Stipend	Music	General Purposes	Hall Upkeep
1870	352	72	95	46	240	82	86	—
1880	484	63	62	59	510	111	93	—
1890	332	58	72	199	332	86	170	67
1900	333	90	15	280	435	116	184	56
1910	259	114	63	515	387	200	142	142
1920	442	99	165	1086	590	183	180	360
1930	454	70	351	830	917	301	346	382
1940	434	59	219	632	794	260	347	7
1950	820	70	659	—	735	198	524	—
1960	976	58	1395	3516	1268	276	768	1120
1970	869	34	624	5180	2297	599	945	2270
1980	3761	129	2400	7971	4490	685	2000	4932

To facilitate comparison over the years an estimate of these amounts has been made in 1980 £'s (see Appendix). While such a calculation must be treated with caution it helps to convey some impression of the trend over the years.

Year	INCOME				EXPENDITURE			
	Stipend	Music	General Purposes	Rents	Stipend	Music	General Purposes	Hall Upkeep
1870	7758	1586	2093	1013	5289	1087	1895	—
1880	11204	1458	1435	1365	11806	2569	2152	—
1890	8983	1569	1948	5384	8983	2327	4600	1813
1900	8824	2385	397	7420	11527	3074	4875	1484
1910	6576	2894	1599	13075	9825	5078	3605	3605
1920	4658	1043	1739	11446	6218	1928	1897	3794
1930	6828	1052	5279	12483	13791	4527	5203	5745
1940	6605	897	3333	9619	12084	3957	5821	106
1950	6084	519	4889	—	5453	1469	3888	—
1960	5202	309	7435	18740	6758	1471	4093	5969
1970	3137	122	2252	18699	8292	2162	3411	8194
1980	3761	129	2400	7971	4490	685	2000	4932

These calculations indicate the extent to which in real terms, income and expenditure have decreased, and the increasing extent to which the congregation has depended on income from property in recent years.

In 1761 it was decided that the accounts for stipend and "poor money" be separated and a treasurer appointed for each fund. This implies that Sunday collections were used then for charitable purposes. After the congregation established the day school it seems that Sunday collections were devoted to its support for in 1868 it was agreed that since the schools were now self supporting the practice of taking collection in the pews after the sermon be discontinued and collection boxes placed in the vestibule. However in 1878 the treasurer drew attention to the decline in the amount collected by this method and recommended reversion to the former practice. This was agreed and the long handled "ladles" used again. In 1880 Mr. F.D. Ward presented a set of collection plates which are still in use. A further complaint is recorded about collections when in 1908 it was stated in the annual report that "Our annual offertory, when compared with the totals raised by other Churches, is very far below what it ought to be" and goes on to point out "23 Presbyterian Churches collect more in one year than we do in five".

During all this period special collections were taken for specific purposes such as the poor house and hospitals as shown by the acknowledgement lists frequently pasted into the minute books. A peculiar minute in 1894 records the committee's decision to cease the practice of interrupting the service to announce the amount of the collection, but to display it instead on a card in the vestibule. There is no indication when this practice started or for how long it was in operation. In 1892 a Church Benevolent Fund was established to enable the minister, in conjunction with the Ladies Committee, to assist the poor of the congregation. It was to be supported by quarterly collections.

In the early days there were two stipend collectors attending to separate areas of the church, who apparently operated in the church vestibule on the first Sunday of each month prior to 1816 when it was changed to the first Sunday in each quarter. This practice was unfavourably commented on in 1880. The collectors received a commission of 5% of their takings, a practice which continued until 1919 when Mr. J.G. Blair was appointed and insisted on acting in an honorary capacity. The church secretary was also paid a fee. This practice continued until the hall was destroyed in 1941 but as the secretary also handled hall lettings it was no doubt for this reason that the fee was paid in the latter years.

In 1922 the Surveyor of Income Tax asked to be supplied with details of the income from the Central Hall so that tax could be assessed. After a prolonged discussion over the next year or two the Tax Inspector agreed that tax was not payable. The treasurer then requested a refund of the tax already paid whereupon the Inspector reconsidered the matter and reimposed tax. The church appealed to the Tax commissioners but lost their case. They then took the matter to Court and obtained a ruling from the Recorder of Belfast for tax exemption which set a precedent for similar cases. During this period it was thought to be advantageous, if tax were payable, to form a separate limited liability company which would be responsible for lettings, and the Central Hall Company Ltd., was formed in 1926. However after the Recorder's decision the Company was of little significance and acted as such in only a few instances. The hall was managed directly by the church committee of which directors of the company were usually members. The company was finally wound up in 1958.

While church funds have been managed with considerable skill over the years there were two decisions which turned out in retrospect to have been unfortunate and worth bearing in mind for the future. These were the long leases granted for the old manse premises in 1799 and of the Skipper Street premises in 1861. While they may have seemed advantageous at the time, particularly in avoiding the need to raise capital and the day-to-day responsibilities for property, subsequent inflation seriously eroded the value of the fixed rents. A list of bequests is given in the appendix. Conditions applied to these varied. Some were available for immediate use and others were to be invested and the income applied to some particular purpose.

Old Communion Plate   *(Reproduced from p 17 Historic Memorials)*

CHAPTER 4   CHURCH SERVICES

There is no record of the number or form of church services in the eighteenth or early nineteenth centuries but some deductions can be made from the occasional references to changes. In 1765 when it was agreed to take a collection of one month's stipend for repairs it was decided that notice would be given thrice on Sunday but it is not clear whether this implies three services on that Sunday. The congregation observed in February 1792 that Dr. Bruce suffered from a severe cold and other complaints and requested him to preach only once on Sunday at 1 o'clock, agreeing that they would be content with such supplies as he can procure for the morning service. In 1805 when the Second Congregation installed an organ the committee decided to consult Heads of Families on the propriety of changing the hours of worship from 12 noon to 1 o'clock and from 2 to 3 o'clock. When it was agreed in 1811 to grant the use of the meeting house to the Rev. E. May when St. George's was being rebuilt, it was decided that service for the use of this congregation to be confined to one at 11 a.m. so that the meeting house would be available for Mr. May's congregation from 12.30 p.m. onwards. There is also a reference at this period to holding committee meetings between the first and second service. So the indications are of two services; the first at 11 a.m. or 12 noon and the second at 1 or 2 o'clock.

There are few references to the length of services but if the church could be ready at 12.30 p.m. for Mr. May's congregation following a service which commenced at 11 o'clock., that service could not have lasted much more than one hour. There is one rather petulant minute of a committee meeting in 1839 which seems to indicate that the congregation was not accustomed to the lengthy sermons said to be common at that time. It reads "Several members attended, but in consequence of the length of the Morning Service by the Rev. Mr. Armstrong, little time remained for business and the meeting was adjourned to the following Sunday". The Unitarian Society had been given the use of the church that day for special services to be conducted by the Rev. George Armstrong of Bristol.

The first reference to an evening service was in September 1827 when it was resolved that there be no evening service in this House on this day fortnight being the day appointed for the opening of the new presbyterian meeting house in Fisherwick Place. But it seems highly probable that the term "evening" was used instead of "afternoon" in this instance. In 1824 the Rev. W. Bruce had given notice of his intention to begin lecturing on August 15th at 6.00 p.m.

There is a record of the committee agreeing on two occasions, in 1830 and 1837, to the meeting house being made available to the ministers of the First and Second Congregations for evening lectures. These seem to have been held in the two houses in alternate years and confined to the summer months until 1834 when, according to Shannon Millen (18), the evening lectures which had been commenced in 1822 were extended to the winter months "the House to be lighted with candles". In 1835 the committee of the First Church decided to install gas lighting for evening services.

In a report to Presbytery in 1838 it is stated that a series of Doctrinal Discourses delivered by Dr. Bruce in 1824 had been published and that in 1829 it was decided to institute a course of Sunday evening lectures for the discussion of controversial subjects and that these had continued since, alternately with the Second Congregation. In the annual report for 1863 there is a reference to a successful series of Sunday evening lectures by the Rev. Scott Porter, the Rev. Dr. Montgomery and the Rev. C.J. McAlester and continues "one mid-day service has been carried out every Lord's Day throughout the year the attendance at which has been, in general, very good".

In the conditions of appointment of Mr. Carroll as organist in 1864 it is stated that he will be required to play at the morning service and an occasional evening service. The annual report for 1878 records:

"since the first Sunday in January an Evening Service at 7.30 has been regularly conducted by the Junior Minister (Mr. Gordon) . . . It is intended to pursue the experiment throughout the summer months. The hour of service from this date will be 7 p.m.".

This reads as though a normal type of service in the evening was an innovation.

The inference is that the second service, which had been an afternoon event in the eighteenth and early nineteenth centuries, was replaced about the third decade of the nineteenth century by afternoon, and later, evening lectures perhaps interspersed with some normal services, or perhaps the term "lecture" meant a service in which the sermon was the prominent feature. The evening service at 7 p.m. seems to have been firmly established at the beginning of the twentieth century, for on several occasions it was agreed that evening service be discontinued during the summer months. It was continued regularly until 1971 when unsettled conditions in the city, interrupting transport services, led to such frequent cancellation of the service that it was decided to abandon it entirely rather than risk inconvenience or even injury to members who felt it their duty to attend if a service was held.

During recent decades the pulpit has been occupied frequently by women but this was a rare occurrence even half a century ago. The first recorded occasion was in 1879 when a service was conducted by Mrs. Caroline A. Soule and the next in 1923 when the Rev. Rosalind Lee preached. Mrs. A.B. Woodhouse of Manchester conducted a service in 1930.

There are very few references in the records to the order of service and those that exist indicate remarkably little change over the years. In 1866 the following order was adopted, presumably differing in some way from that previously in use, but the nature of the change is not given;

Chant
Prayer
First Lesson
Hymn
Prayer
Second Lesson
Anthem
Sermon
Hymn
Prayer

Forty years later when the evening service had become an established practice and after the new organ was installed, the order for the two services was:

MORNING	EVENING
Voluntary	Voluntary
Chant	Introit
Prayer	Prayer
First Lesson	Hymn
Hymn	First Lesson
Second Lesson	Anthem
Hymn	Second Lesson
Prayer	Hymn
Anthem	Address

Sermon	Organ Solo and collection
Notices	Anthem
Hymn	Hymn
Lord's Prayer	Lord's Prayer (chanted)
Benediction	Benediction

The paucity of reference in the records to the order of service was probably due mainly to a lack of any great desire for change, but was also influenced by the view of some members that the order of service was a matter for the minister to decide; not the committee.

The one occasion when this question arose was at a special joint meeting of the general and music committees on 4 August 1867 which had been requisitioned to consider this matter. The Rev. Scott Porter reported to this meeting that since he became sole minister the previous May he had altered the order agreed in 1866 (quoted above) by placing the second lesson immediately after the first lesson — otherwise it remained the same. The joint committees resolved:

"That having taken into consideration the order of services of Public worship as conducted by Mr. Porter since the first Sunday in May we hereby approve of the same, trusting that it will not be departed from unless peculiar circumstances shall in the opinion of the minister officiating render a deviation necessary".

At the next meeting of the committee a letter was read from Mr. W.J.C. Allen, treasurer, and it is recorded that:

"In his letter Mr. Allen stated that he entertained a strong opinion on the principle involved in the resolution passed at the last quarterly meeting which he conceived was the assertion of a right to control the minister in the discharge of his pulpit duties and consequently he had determined upon resigning his office of Treasurer".

The committee agreed not to discuss the matter at that meeting because of poor attendance but appointed Mr. McClelland, Mr. Harland and the secretary to wait upon Mr. Allen. At the next meeting the deputation reported:

"that at the request of several members of the Congregation for whom he had a high respect he (Mr. Allen) on receiving their explanations in writing to prevent any symptom of disunion had consented to withdraw his resignation of the Treasurership".

This apparently settled the matter as there is no further reference to it. Curiously no one seems to have suggested that it was a matter for the minister to settle in conjunction with the committee acting as a session, though in effect this was what the committee had done. Such changes as have been made from time to time have faded out and the basic pattern remains the same. For example in 1929 it was decided to have a liturgical form of service with choral responses once each month but it continued for only a short time.

While the order for ordinary services appears to have continued with little change over the years, the order for special services such as at Christmas, Palm Sunday, Harvest Thanksgiving and other special occasions, has been devised to suit each occasion. It is not at all clear from the records when these various special services were first introduced or how they have evolved over the years, but some references are interesting. In 1913 it was agreed to have a Carol Service at Christmas "same as last year" but how long it had been the practice before this is not known. In 1948 the organist referred to a service of carols and readings as a new venture but there are references to carols in the intervening years. The carol service by candlelight which is now an established occasion of the year was introduced by the Rev. Dr. McLachlan in 1955. In 1976 it was agreed to invite the members of St. Mary's Roman Catholic Church of Chapel Lane, and St. George's Church of Ireland in High Street, to share in this carol service and this joint and happy venture has continued ever since. The first reference to a Christmas tree in the Church is in 1922.

In the calendar for June 1944 it is stated that the first harvest thanksgiving service was held in 1881 and the first reference in the records to one occurs in that year. It may well have been the first as the committee gave approval for it in that year, so there must have been some unusual reason for raising the matter in committee. In 1906 the committee directed that nails were not to be driven into the woodwork for harvest decoration. A Christmas Day service held in 1947 was referred to as an innovation but the term is more likely to have been used in relation to the immediate past than the whole history of the congregation.

Communion services appear to have been held half yearly all through the history of the congregation though Adair refers to quarterly communion services in Co. Down in the early years of the seventeenth century. In the nineteenth century there appears to have been two pre-communion services and one post-communion service on weekdays. In 1818 it was agreed to accept a proposal from the Second Congregation that Thursday be fixed as one of the days of public worship before communion (instead of Wednesday) and to a change of the time of the service on the Monday after communion. Whether the two congregations held joint services is not clear but seems likely. It is on record that the pre-communion services in 1877 were on Thursday at 8 p.m. and Saturday at 2 p.m. The Saturday service was also held at 11.30 a.m. some years. There is no reference to a post-communion service at this period.

A proposal to discontinue pre-communion services in view of the poor attendance was discussed in 1898 but it was agreed to hold one more to test the attendance. After this test the minister reported poor attendance again, but "as there were adverse circumstances" it was agreed to have another trial. The committee was obviously reluctant to allow the practice to lapse. A list of services given in annual reports shows a pre-communion service on Wednesday evenings up to 1906, after which it is referred to as a "Preparation Class" held in the vestry.

In 1809 it was agreed to provide an additional table and forms for each aisle for communion because of the increased numbers and in a report to Presbytery in 1838 it was stated that the usual number for the communion service was about 200. A reference to communion in the minutes of a meeting in November 1837 suggests that four tables were used with four deacons at each but in the 1860's a number of references suggest three tables for each aisle with two deacons for each table i.e. a total of twelve deacons.

New arrangements for communion are described in the annual report for 1873:

"by way of experiment, it has been determined that instead of requiring communicants to leave their seats and take their places on benches placed in the aisles, the bread and wine will be carried to them while seated in their respective pews, and will be distributed among them by the officiating Deacons. This will enable the whole Congregation to communicate at one time; will prevent the confusion and inconvenience which so frequently arise in the act of approaching and leaving the tables; will obviate the necessity of repeated celebrations and addresses; and will put it in the power of the whole Congregation to remain till the close of the service".

This conveys an impression of the form of communion service prior to that date. Apparently the experiment was regarded as a success, for the communion linen was divided between the ministers in 1878.

In 1908 it was decided to have a table made similar to the one in the vestry, which had been cleaned and repolished, so that both could be used at communion and placed on glass pedastals to raise them to a suitable height to suit the six deacons who occupied the bench seat. The other six deacons sat on chairs. Concern was expressed in 1917 about the small number attending communion services and it was suggested that this could be improved by the use of individual cups. The congregation was polled on this question and 101 voted in favour of individual cups with 17 not in favour. A set of individual glasses was presented to the congregation by Mr. Bowman Malcolm and they were used for the first time in April 1918.

A controversy arose in 1927 about the use of fermented or unfermented wine at communion. Among receipts in the middle of the nineteenth century is an occasional item for half a dozen bottles of finest Port. It is not stated that this wine was purchased for communion but the dates of purchase suggest that it was. According to Reid (4) forty bottles of the best claret were used at the first communion at Templepatrick on 4 July 1647. Opinion about the type of wine to be used was divided in 1927, and for some years following both types of wine (fermented and unfermented) were placed on the trays, labelled so that members could choose. The question was again discussed in 1934 when it was agreed to leave the matter to the minister to settle as he thought proper.

The communion service is open, that is anyone who so desires may attend and participate. No questions are raised about beliefs or membership of any particular church or denomination. It is entirely a matter for individuals to decide for themselves whether the service is significant and helpful. It has been an open service for as long as anyone can remember and there is no indication in the records that it was ever changed from some different procedure in earlier times. In some presbyterian churches it was customary for members of the session to give out tokens to members they considered eligible to take communion but no such tokens have been found in connection with the First Church. However it is probable that the session which existed two centuries ago would have exercised this function and that may well have been one of the reasons why the session as such was allowed to lapse.

The old communion plate has been retained. It consists of two alms dishes dating from 1721, six pewter plates, a silver cup dating from 1693 and six other silver cups and six flagons. A photograph of it is included in Dr. Wilde's 1944 book. It was valued at £256.10.0. in 1928 so the current value must be around £5000. Part of this plate was presented before the division of the First and Second Congregations and some to both after the division. This led to a long correspondence between them about ownership in the early years of the present century which was amicably settled in 1938 by an agreement of joint ownership of several of the pieces.

Since broadcasting was introduced in the third decade of the twentieth century a number of services have been broadcast. These included:

7.12.1924	The Rev. Rossington with the organist and choir broadcast a service from the Belfast studios of the BBC.
30.8.1931	The Rev. R.N. Cross broadcast a service from the studio.
11.6.1933	Evening Service broadcast from the church on the occasion of the 150th Anniversary of the church building.
30.9.1934	Evening Service conducted by Rev. R.N. Cross broadcast from church.
30.1.1938	A service conducted by Rev. R.N. Cross broadcast from studio.
15.5.1949	Morning Service conducted by Rev. Dr. Wilde broadcast from church.
13.2.1955	Evening Service conducted by Rev. Dr. McLachlan broadcast from church.
24.11.1963	Evening Service conducted by Rev. Dr. McLachlan broadcast from church.
15.10.1964	Service recorded by BBC for General Overseas Service.
23.10.1966	Dr. McLachlan conducted a service in the studio for United Nations Day.
1971	Part of service telerecorded by ITV for use in "Aquarius" programme.
7.10.1973	Morning Service conducted by Rev. D.G. Wigmore-Beddoes broadcast from church.
30.10.1977	Morning Service conducted by Rev. D.G. Banham broadcast from church.
7.3.1982	Morning Service conducted by Rev. D.G. Banham broadcast from church.

CHAPTER 5 CHURCH MUSIC

The only reference in the earlier minute books from which inferences can be drawn about the choir and music are to the singing clerk and to boys from the Poor school who sang in the choir. The singing clerk was obviously regarded as an important personage in the congregation and the number of boys mentioned at different times ranged from six to twenty four. There are no references to adult members of the choir until 1808 when William Hughes was appointed singing clerk and he was required "to instruct at least from six to eight young persons to sing in two parts and teach one or two Bass voices". There is no further reference to boys in the choir after the first decade of the nineteenth century, subsequent references being to adults — mainly the engagement of paid singers.

A Bass voice was advertised for in 1816 and in the same year it is recorded that a Mr. McGhie and his family offered to assist with "singing in parts". The first reference to a lady singer was to Mrs. Ann Crooks in 1818 and in the same year a Signor Guarrini was engaged to instruct the choir in singing which perhaps implies a choir consisting of volunteer adults. References since that time suggest that the choir consisted of paid principals with other voluntary members. The only instrumental assistance in the early days was the pitch pipe used by the clerk. At a meeting of Heads of Families in 1801 "a very liberal proposal from Mr. Edward Bunting respecting the purchase of an organ" was considred and it was agreed to request Dr. Bruce to "return their thanks to Mr. Bunting in the warmest terms of gratitude", but apparently they decided against the installation of an organ at that time as the first organ was not installed until 1853. The one then installed was a second-hand instrument and apparently not very satisfactory as it had to be replaced by a new one in 1855. At that time the organ and choir were located in the gallery but had to be removed to ground level half a century later when the new organ presented by the Misses Riddel could not be intalled in the gallery.

In the earlier years the music seems to have consisted of singing psalms in the form of chants. There is nothing in the records to suggest that the singing of psalms in the paraphrased form to hymn tunes was ever adopted in the congregation.

From the commencement of the first minute book (1760) until 1801 there is no reference to a psalm or tune book, then at a committee meeting on 3 May 1801 it is recorded that, "Dr. Bruce having proposed to make a new collection of psalms for the use of this congregation, the proposal was accepted." Eleven hundred copies were published and went on sale in January 1802. By May 1816 this psalm book was out of print and it was proposed that it be reprinted "with such alterations and additions as Dr. Bruce may please to adopt." Dr. Bruce was instructed to inform the Second Congregation that a new edition of the psalms was about to be printed "and to learn if they will adopt the new one." An advertisement was approved to be inserted in the Belfast newspapers; "Shortly will be published a new edition (considerably enlarged and improved) of the psalms, hymns and spiritual songs at present used by the First and Second Congregations of Presbyterians in Belfast . . ." and offering its use to "any Society or individuals" who wished to order it. This presumably was an attempt, in the interests of economy, to provide something suitable to both congregations as only the psalms were in use in the First Congregation.

During this period there is no indication as to the source of the tunes used in the singing of the psalms. In April 1815 the committee ordered "that Mr. Joy procure a firm in Dublin and engage on the part of this committee to pay Mr. Goodwin of that city, engraver, a sum not exceeding £10 on the completion of plates of a new Book of Psalm Tunes prepared by Mr. Hughes." but there is no further reference to this transaction. At the annual meeting on 13 June 1819 it was resolved "That the Musical Committee be requested to see the music is regulated in point of compass as in every psalm to suit the voices of the congregation."

When William Hughes returned to the church as singing clerk in August 1819, as part of his duties he was required "to write out all music that may be necessary for the choir." It was also stipulated that "no tunes at present in the use of the House shall be thrown out, nor any new ones introduced without the previous sanction of the Musical Committee." From this we may safely deduce that no published tune book was in use. Tunes culled from various sources were in manuscript form for the use of the choir only; the congregation coping as best it could. This is confirmed by a committee resolution of January 1825; "As some members of the congregation are desirous of improving the psalmody, the Committee are of opinion that Mr. Hughes should attend at the hours that should be agreed upon". In February of the same year, the treasurer was requested to pay £2.10.0 to Mr. Hughes, "so soon as he shall produce a complete copy of the present psalmody of the House, written out in score." This was produced by Hughes in April and on the instructions of the committee was "to be neatly bound." Unfortunately no trace can be found of this volume nor of five psalm tunes composed by Hughes for which the music committee recommended that he be paid £5.

Considerable changes took place in the music of the church during the period of the missing minute book. An organ had been introduced into the church and hymn singing had become part of the worship. The terms of appointment applicable to the first organist in 1853 specified that "The Musical Committee alone has the right of sanctioning any alterations in the collection of psalm tunes, doxologies and anthems now in use in the congregation or in the arrangements of the tunes contained in it." At first sight this might be taken to indicate the existence of a published collection in use in the church. However, the same terms of appointment applied in February 1864 when Mr. B. Hobson Carroll became organist and yet, in April 1865 at the annual meeting it was reported that the music committee had made a selection of anthems and doxologies, the words of which it was proposed to print for use in the religious services. No reference is made to an earlier publication. The book became available in May 1866 under the title "Chants, Anthems and Doxologies for the use of the First Presbyterian Congregation, Belfast." It contains the words of the chants with a preface on how they should be sung. The words of 120 anthems and doxologies are also given, a few of which are still sung in the church, e.g. 'Turn Thy Face from my Sins' — Attwood; 'Thou Visitest The Earth' — Greene; and three by Farrant, 'Call to Remembrance', 'Hide Not Thou Thy Face' and 'Lord For Thy Tender Mercies Sake'.

In July, 1869 a report by the Rev. John Scott Porter and Mr. B. Hobson Carroll was made to the committee on the publication of hymns suitable for the use of the congregation. It refers to the lack of a proper hymn book containing the hymn tunes used in the church, "the great majority of the tunes used being taken from the manuscript collection which has for many years been employed in our singing desk, compiled at a time when the members of the congregation were not expected — scarcely even were wished — to join in the psalmody" and containing many tunes "which from their intricacy and difficulty could only be performed in a satisfactory manner by a trained professional choir; and the use of which would condemn to silence many whose voices would gladly join in simpler melodies."

The aim was now to encourage the congregation to join more in the singing of the hymns by providing them with a hymn book which they "could procure for themselves, use in the pews, take home to their families and practice during the week." Despite the tremendous amount of work put into the report (producing a final selection of 104 tunes) the committee did not take any action on it until November 1871 when "it was agreed that the Hymn Tunes be printed in condensed score", and in the annual report of March 1873 it is stated that "The Collection of Sacred Melodies compiled by your Committee . . . has been published." By January, 1877 no copies of this hymn book were available so the committee was asked to consider reprinting it or compiling another. It was January, 1880 before they gave their approval for the printing of a new collection and the Rev. Porter was requested "to prepare a manuscript of the proposed hymn book." However it does not appear that this was ever proceeded with as no further reference to it appears in the minutes.

In April 1884 the music committee sanctioned the use of 'The Sunday Scholars Hymn Book' in the evening services with the object of encouraging the Sunday school scholars and their parents to attend evening services. (These had been commenced on a regular-basis in January, 1877). The committee also santioned the introduction of a third hymn at the evening service.

The annual report of 1885 — 6 reported that "The Revised Hymnal undertaken by the Non-Subscribing Association is now ready for the press . . . the best hymns in our existing collection are carefully incorporated in this new collection of some 420 hymns". These were apparently words only as, in September 1886, Dr. Carroll proposed at the music committee that "if the new hymn book be adopted, a number of copies of the 'Bristol Tune Book' and 'Irish Church Hymnal' be purchased for the Choir. The 'Hymns for Christian Worship' was approved to come into use on Sunday the 5 December 1886.

A revised edition of 'Chants and Anthems' was brought into use in October, 1889. As before, it contains an explanatory note on the singing of chants but in this edition bar lines have been introduced. The number of anthems has been reduced to 90. It should be explained that the choir was restricted to the singing only of these anthems at the normal Sunday services. The permission of the music committee had to be obtained if the organist wished to introduce a new anthem at, for example, Harvest or Easter. Thus in March, 1892 we find Mr. Stewart applying for permission "to occasionally use some of the anthems which are not in the Anthem Book, and to have a little extra music". The committee replied that they "will sanction a vocal instead of an instrumental voluntary at morning service, during the collection on the first Sunday of each calendar month. During other Sundays the regular instrumental form to be adhered to."

This is a good example of the strict control exercised by the music committee at that time. The music was intended to be secondary to the other parts of the service — an understandable sentiment but one which must have been frustrating to both organist and choir. When Dr. Carroll's services were terminated in 1888 the opportunity was taken to draft a new set of rules for subsequent organists. There were set out in a formal legal document which the organist had to sign before a witness. Clause 11 in particular, reads like an extract from an Act of Parliament: "The Music Committee reserves to themselves the right from time to time of varying, cancelling or adding to all or any of the foregoing articles. Notice in writing thereof containing the particulars given or sent to the organist signed by the Secretary or two members of the Music Committee which shall be conclusive evidence of the variation, cancellation or addition having been duly made as aforesaid and shall be thereupon binding and conclusive upon the organist as if originally included in the articles."

However, it should be said in fairness that during the time of B. Hobson Carroll as organist, he and the choir were given other opportunities to display their abilities. At the installation of the Rev. Alexander Gordon, M.A., on the 5 June 1877, a soiree was held in the evening in the Music Hall, May Street at which the choir sang an anthem and two part songs. The following year it was decided that the annual meeting should take the form of a meeting followed by refreshments and entertainment. This became the regular format, the choir singing part songs; members of the choir (paid and voluntary) singing duets and solos and Mr. Carroll accompanying and contributing solos on the piano. At the re-opening of the church on 9 October, 1881 following alterations and re-decoration, Mr. Carroll was requested to prepare special music, details of which were reported in the *Northern Whig* of the following day. Mr. Carroll played one of his own compositions as opening voluntary, 'Adagio Cantabile (Septuor)' by Beethoven during the service and 'Splendente Te Deus' by Mozart as his closing voluntary. The choir sang 'I was Glad' — Sir George Elvey and the 'Hallelujah' chorus from Handel's 'Messiah'.

At the Centennial of the present meeting house a conversazione was held in the Ulster Hall on the 20 June, 1883 and Mr. Carroll obviously took full advantage of being able to play a much superior organ than he was used to. The *Northern Whig* reports that "from 6.00 p.m. to 7.30 p.m. Mr. Carroll performed the following items in excellent style upon the organ; Overture L'Italiane in Algeria (Rossini); 'Coronation March, Le Prophete' (Meyerbeer); 'Fantasia for the organ, "Erin" (B.H. Carroll); 'Bacarolle' (Spohr); 'Andante in G' (Batiste) and 'Triumphal March, Naaman' (Costa)." An augmented choir (described as The Centennial Choir) led the hymn singing and sang the anthem 'Hear my Prayer' by Mendelssohn. Three other choir items and one solo completed a not insignificant musical contribution. For the opening of the old Central Hall on 14 January 1886 Dr Carroll composed a sacred cantata in addition to which the choir sang four part songs one of which was also composed by Dr. Carroll.

Dr. Carroll did much to establish the musical tradition which succeeding organists were to build upon but his long period as organist, covering twenty four years was not to be equalled until Albert Taylor came in 1918 and remained for thirty two years. The fact that there were twelve organists in the thirty years between Dr. Carroll's departure and Mr. Taylor's arrival suggests an uneasy relationship between the organists and committee at this time. There was no shortage of organists at this period for on several occasions over twenty applications were received in response to advertisement, some from apparently well qualified musicians.

As with all societies there were differences of opinion about the priorities to be given to the allocation of funds, and the organists, supported by music lovers in the congregation, often pressed the committee for more generous provision for music. At this time there were many reports on the poor state of the organ, and organists sometimes initiated fund raising ventures which were not always appreciated. One rather outstanding example was in January 1896 when the committee was informed by the treasurer that he had received a cheque for £4.4.0. from Messrs. Harland & Wolff enclosed with an account which had been issued by the organist for "Professional services of Choir and Organist on the occasion of funeral (as usual)". This was Sir. E.J. Harland's funeral. The committee hastily decided to return the cheque with a letter of apology, and issued strict instructions to the organist not to issue any such accounts in future.

The strict control by the music committee over choice of music to be performed was gradually relaxed in the first decades of the twentieth century being replaced by the present practice where the organist makes his own choice of music. The only example of a change from the organist's choice in this century was early in Mr. Taylor's career when he readily agreed, on the music committee's suggestion, to substitute part three of the Messiah for "From Olivet to Calvary" which he had proposed.

The problem of the condition of the organ was resolved when the new Lęwis organ was installed in 1907, a transaction for which Mr. Alfred Hollins acted as consultant. This gave a new impetus to the musical side of the service, the order of which was revised and extended at this time. Organ recitals on weekday evenings also became popular.   For example one given by Mr. Hollins on Monday 11 March 1907 included:

Fugue in E flat	Bach
Larghetto from Clarinet Quintette	Mozart
Priere et Berceuse	Guilmant
Pastorale	Lemare
Humoresque	Dvorak
Scherzo	Turner

and another by Arthur Davis (the church organist) on Wednesday 16 October 1907 included:

Toccata and Fugue in D Minor	Bach
Barcarolle	Hoffman
Funeral March and Hymn of Seraphs	Guilmant
Suite Gothique	Boellmann
In Paradisum	Dubois
Concert Overture in C	Hollins

These recitals continued for a number of years.

Special musical occasions during the year include Palm Sunday, Church Anniversary, Harvest Festival and Christmas. There has also been a Music Sunday for many years to which local school choirs and orchestras, particularly Methodist College, have frequently been invited. Among the various works (or excerpts from them) mentioned in the records as having been performed on such occasions are:

Gaul:	Holy City
Bach:	Passion (St. John)
Mendelssohn:	Hymn of Praise
Haydn:	Creation

Bach:	Christmas Oratorio
Wagner:	Selection from Parsifal
Stainer:	Crucifixion
Handel:	Messiah
Palestrina:	Missa Aeterne Christe Munera
Britten:	Rejoice in the Lamb
Kodaly:	Jesus and the Traders
Bach:	Magnificat
Byrd:	Mass for four voices
Britten:	Festival Te Deum
Vivaldi:	The Gloria
Faure:	Requiem
Haydn:	The Nelson Mass
Bach:	Cantata No. 140. Sleepers Wake
	Cantata No. 112. The Lord is my Shepherd.

During the 1930s the B.B.C. broadcast from the church mid-day organ recitals by Mr. Albert Taylor for several years, and in recent years the present organist, Mr. R.A. Megraw, has given mid-day organ recitals during the summer for shoppers and those who work in the city centre.

A copy of an article by Mr. W.H. McCafferty entitled *Psalmody of the Old Congregation of Belfast 1760—1840* published by the Unitarian Historical Society is pasted into minute book No. 12 at page 298, and an account of church music with a description of the organ by Mr. Albert Taylor is included in *Three Hundred Years of Worship, Work and Witness.*

Church Interior 1983   *Photo: Philip McConnell*

CHAPTER 6   SUNDAY SCHOOL AND LIBRARY

The first reference to a Sunday school in the records was in 1833 when the ministers of the First and Second congregations recommended the establishment of Sunday schools, probably as a consequence of the recent establishment of the Remonstrant Synod of Ulster. It is not clear whether it was to be a joint school for both congregations but in any case no action was taken for another five years. The First congregation's Sunday school opened on 28 January 1838 with 70 pupils and 20 teachers on the first day. A return made to the Presbytery in 1838 gives the average attendance at Sunday school as 43 for Boys and 61 for girls and the times at which the school was held was from 9.30 to 10.30 a.m. and 2.30 to 4.00 p.m. It seems probable that a different set of teachers attended the morning and afternoon sessions. There is little information about the Sunday school during the period of the missing minute book but in 1863 reference is made to a Junior Minister's class having 37 on the roll with an average attendance of 21. This class apparently met on Sunday mornings from 10 to 11 a.m.

In the annual report for 1871 it is stated that:

"The minister has resumed his weekly meetings with the younger members of the congregation. About forty of these attend a class held on Wednesday evenings at his own house, and nearly as many more come to his Sunday School each Lord's Day in the Fountain Street schoolroom".

And in the 1874 annual report:

"This year our Pastor, instead of resuming the Minister's Class which he had personally conducted for several years past, availed himself of the assistance of some of the young persons belonging to the congregation, who kindly consented to act as Teachers in a Congregational Sunday School. Besides Mr. Porter, six ladies and gentlemen have taken charge of classes".

This arrangement commenced in December 1873 and there were 48 pupils on the roll with an average attendance of 36.

It is not clear where this school met — possibly in the Fountain Street school but there seems to have been some difficulty about using it for in August 1883 an agreement was made with a Mr. Barron for a room for the Sunday school in his building in Royal Avenue with an entrance from Garfield Street. The records at this period suggest a discussion in the congregation about the propriety of a Sunday school as there seems to have been some

100

objection to any kind of denominational instruction. Whatever the context of the discussion the outcome was agreement that the curriculum of the Sunday school should include:

"not only our own denominational views but the Christian religion in its historic character as compared, and in relation to, the religions of the world".

Apparently medals were issued in connection with the Sunday school as the secretary displayed one in a committee meeting in 1902. He had obtained the medal from Mr. Shannon Millen and it was described as having on the obverse side a bust of Christ with the inscription "Salvator Mundi" and on the reverse "First Presbyterian Congregation Sunday School". At a later meeting Mr. Walmsley told the committee that from enquiries he had made these medals had been issued prior to 1886 after which date books were issued to pupils instead — presumably as prizes.

When the Central Hall was completed in 1885 there was adequate accommodation for the Sunday School and it has continued ever since. The number of pupils seems to have fluctuated quite widely from occasional figures which appear in the record; thus 73 is given as the number enrolled in 1873; 32 in 1878; 80 in 1884; 135 in 1889; 98 in 1898; 80 in 1908; 100 in 1912 and 65 in 1919. The activities of the Sunday school were of course restricted as the population moved away from the centre of the city and modern traffic conditions prevented young children from coming to church unless escorted. In 1945 it was decided to have Sunday school at the same time as morning service so that children could travel with their parents.

Library

It was agreed in 1837 to establish a lending library for the use of members who could change books after service on Sundays. It was opened in 1838 with Mr. Wm. Hartley as librarian. New books were purchased from time to time and the titles purchased towards the end of the nineteenth century were frequently published in the annual reports. A number of catalogues of library books was produced from time to time. The years of publication mentioned in the records include 1846, 1869, 1876 and 1894 but there may have been others.

By 1890 there were over 1000 volumes in the library and during that year 38 members had taken out 160 books. This was said to be a very much reduced use of the library compared with former years and raised the question of the value of the library to the congregation. However in 1903 it was decided that in spite of the fact that books were now freely available from other libraries in the city, the usefulness of the congregational library was not yet past. (The Free Library Act was passed in 1882 and the foundation stone for the Belfast Free Library laid in 1884). In 1926 an effort was made to revive the activity of the library by arranging for members of the library committee to be available in the library after service to issue books to members. The library committee which had existed from 1890 disappeared in 1928 though librarians continued to be appointed each year until 1962.

In 1868 Mrs. Bruce presented the Rev. William Bruce's theological books to the church to form a Minister's library to be kept separate from the congregational library. In 1900 these books were presented to Queen's College with the request that they be added to the Antrim library which had been presented to the College in 1873 by the Presbytery of Antrim. The College was unable to arrange this but provided a small label to be pasted into each book to maintain identification. There is also reference in the records to a Sunday school library which was apparently maintained separately for the use of the Sunday school.

The books in the library had to be removed to the Central Hall during the repair of bomb damage to the church in 1975. In 1978 they were returned to the session room, sorted and catalogued by a team of volunteers under Mr. Banham's guidance. At the same time books presented by Mrs. Wigmore-Beddoes, Mrs. Amy Castellano and the Rev. J. Radcliffe were incorporated with the existing stock. Some valuable books were sold by Dr. McLachlan in 1956 to raise funds for the appeal for the rebuilding of the Central Hall and in 1979 Mr. J.W. Vitty M.A., formerly librarian of the Linen Hall library, examined some of the older volumes considered to be no longer of interest to members, and selected a number of volumes for sale.

CHAPTER 7 THE CHURCH AND SCHOOLS

During its long history the congregation has been closely associated with the development of various educational institutions in the City of Belfast. One of the earliest schools in the city was David Manson's school which opened in Clugston's Entry (Lombard Street) in 1775 and later moved to several other sites including Donegall Street. Manson's name appears in the 1775 and 1790 lists of members.

There are many references in the first minute book to a school referred to as the Poor school or Charity school which seems to have existed in connection with the Charitable Institution which had been established in the middle of the eighteenth century. In 1782 the committee resolved "that as many members of the committee who could do so would meet in the Vestry with the two ministers at 12 noon on the first Wednesday of each month to inspect the state of the school and that the master shall attend and report on the boys". In August 1766 the committee ordered that Mr. Crawford (the teacher) make a report every month and such boys as are idle, do not attend or will not learn to read and write shall be called before the committee and discharged. Four boys were discharged at that meeting and it was agreed that in future no boy be admitted unless recommended by a member of the committee. In 1771 Mr. Crawford emigrated to America but his wife carried on the school and in 1775 she, with another teacher, appeared with the boys who were examined by members of the committee in singing, reading etc.

At one of the meetings in the Vestry at which the affairs of the school were considered eleven boys were named to receive free "cloathes" but some others were excluded because of poor attendance or bad behaviour. It was stipulated that parents or friends should give proper security for the "cloaths". At a later meeting some boys who had been discharged were re-admitted and it was directed that they should be "cloathed" but these "cloaths" were to be left in the vestry after services on Sundays. On one occasion it was decided that Mr. Vincent (singing clerk in the church) should instruct two boys to "raise the psalm tunes" so as to be able to take Mr. Vincent's place on Sundays in case of indisposition. In 1796 Ernest Cochrane (singing clerk) was directed to purchase shoes for six children who sang with him, the treasurer to pay the bill. There were also frequent bills for baps for the school children.

It is clear that some of the boys came to the church on Sundays to sing in the choir but whether the "cloaths" and other attention were confined to these or applied to the school generally is not clear. This close association between the school and the congregation appears to have ended in the early years of the nineteenth century.

At the annual meeting of the congregation in 1839 it was reported that an evening school had been opened by six young gentlemen of the congregation for boys who wished to learn reading, writing and counting. It was held on two evenings each week and the average attendance ranged from 25 to 35.

Concurrent with this interest in primary education in the eighteenth century the congregation was deeply involved with the foundation of Belfast Academy of which the Rev. Dr. Crombie was the first principal. He was succeeded by the Rev. Dr. Bruce who also succeeded him as minister in the First Church, and for a long time it was popularly referred to as "Dr. Bruce's Academy". In 1811 there is a reference in the record to a pew occupied by Academy boarders and in 1822 Dr. Bruce wrote to the committee thanking them for the use of a pew for pupils of "his" Academy.

Members of the congregation were also deeply involved in the establishment of the Academical Institution, in spite of the attitude attributed to Dr. Bruce that there was no need for another establishment for higher education in Belfast. Of the 66 subscribers named in the Act twelve appear in the list of First Church members and five of the twenty original managers were members (three of them members of the committee) as well as the first treasurer of Inst — Robert Calwell.

Church members appear on the list of governors over the years and many of the teachers in the early days were members of the congregation including Rev. Dr. T.D. Hincks, Rev. Dr. H. Montgomery, Dr. T. Blain, Dr. W. Burden, Dr. J. Burden, John Carlisle and Randal C. Nixon. The Rev. Wm. Bruce, junior minister of the congregation, was appointed Professor of Greek and Hebrew in the Institution in 1821 against strong opposition on account of his religious connections. It was said that the governors appointed him to gain the favour of Lord Castlereagh (a friend of Bruce's father) in order to secure restoration of the government grant which had been withdrawn from the Institution because some of the teachers were suspected of holding anti-government views. The Rev. J. Scott Porter served as secretary to the Governors for a period and later as Professor of Divinity. W.J.C. Allen who was secretary of the school for a lengthy period was a prominent member of the congregation and another member John Rogers, was chairman of the Board of Governors for many years. Lady Pirrie was President of the School from 1931 to 1935.

Dr. Wm. Drennan delivered the opening address at the Institution in February 1814 and in the course of it referred to the attitude of the management to religion which reflected the influence of the First Church:

"Of nothing are the Boards more desirous, than that pupils of all religious denominations should communicate, by frequent and friendly intercourse, in the common business of education by which means a new turn might be given to the national character and habits, and all the children of Ireland should know and love each other".

A noble sentiment, but in vain, for the first quarter century of Inst's existence was blighted by religious discord. The liberal, non-sectarian status at which the managers aimed was most unpopular in some quarters. It was subjected to bitter attack by the Subscribing Presbyterians led by Dr. Cooke who wanted the projected Collegiate Department to provide education for future ministers on a firm Calvinistic basis.

According to John Jamieson (19) the historian of Inst, Cooke laboured to get the non-subscribers expelled from the Synod of Ulster as a preliminary step in harnessing the full weight of the Synod against the liberal stance adopted by the managers of the school. In the event the school managers stood firm against interference with the religious opinions of teachers or pupils, but had to sacrifice for this principle the projected Collegiate status.

The same problem arose with elementary education after the non-subscribers withdrew from the Synod of Ulster. It was reported that managers of elementary schools were refusing admission to children who attended the First Church Sunday school and so the congregation set about providing not its own denominational school but an undenominational school. The denominationalisation of elementary education is described by Dudley Edwards (20) thus:

"From this time (1831) dates the establishment in Ireland of a national system of education devised by Stanley, the Chief Secretary, based upon an undenominational principle, abandoning the demand of the Established Church that public education must be under its control. Stanley's plan might have succeeded, by educating together the children of all denominations, in terminating the mutual hatreds of Catholicism, Presbyterians and Protestantism. It had the support of O'Connell and of the Catholic and Protestant archbishops of Dublin, Murray and Whately. It was not without some Presbyterian supporters. At first it had no Catholic critics. But the system was to be eroded, first by the Presbyterians, then by some of the Catholics and episcopalians, that it ultimately became controlled by representatives of the three Churches, reorganising the schools on a virtually denominational basis".

In an attempt to arrest this development the congregation decided in 1838 to establish a non-denominational school. It started off with a rented house in Rosemary Street with accommodation for 25 girls but as this was inadequate larger premises were sought. In 1839 a site in King Street was considered but a clear title could not be obtained. In the autumn of 1839 a site was secured in Fountain Street and a school was built and ready for occupation after the summer holiday in 1840. An extract from the Trust Deed of this school reads:

"to permit and suffer the building . . . to be used and occupied as and for a public school in which poor children residing in the Town and neighbourhood of Belfast may receive during the six working days of the week instruction in the usual and necessary branches of an ordinary education free from all interference and control on the part of the teacher or teachers of the said school or of the Trustees herein named and appointed . . . or any other person whomsoever . . . in respect of the religious opinions or tenets which such poor children or their parents or guardians may entertain: it being hereby declared to be the true intent and meaning of these presents and the parties hereto to provide a place to which poor children of every denomination without distinction may be sent for the purpose of receiving a good secular and moral education without reference to the peculiar tenets of any particular sect".

The application to the National Board of Education for recognition of the school stated that the hours are from 10 a.m. to 3 p.m. and that Mrs. Hayes was principal at a salary of £15 per year. The Board agreed to approve the school paying Mrs. Hayes £8 per year and supplying books for the average numbers attending provided that the school was called Fountain Street National School and the name displayed. It is not clear from the record whether the congregation considered vesting the school in the Commissioners or the reasons for not doing so, since their conditions were identical with those specified by the Commissioners for vested schools. This would have enabled them to obtain from the Commissioners a grant of two thirds of the cost of the building and grants for upkeep, and the provision of more generous salaries for the teachers. Of course as Mary McNeill (21) has pointed out in her biography of Vere Foster this low level of salaries for teachers was common throughout Ireland. Even as late as the 1860s "Salaries assured by the Board were rarely more than £30 and often as little as £18 per annum; they were intended merely as a basic wage to be supplemented by voluntary contributions which seldom materialised".

In 1863 the Fountain Street School Trustees (who were appointed by the congregation) converted the property to fee farm grant and acquired an adjoining house, No. 20, to extend the school. Sunday collections were devoted to the schools but in 1868 it was reported that the Fountain Street Schools were now self-supporting, though that did not last long as subsequent appeals were made to the congregation for funds.

A detailed report by the Rev. J. Scott Porter on these schools in 1869 contained the following information: the girls school of which Mrs. Hayes was still principal (since the school commenced in 1838) occupied the upper floor and had an average attendance of 86.2. Mrs. Hayes salary was £73.10.0 per year with a residence. The first assistant, Miss M. Hunter, had £16 per year; the second assistant, Miss I. Smyth, £12. Of the 235 children on the roll 78 were Episcopal Church, 5 Roman Catholic, 144 Presbyterian and 13 other denominations. The children paid 2d per week which raised £28.18.0 in the year. The Infant school, in the lower floor, under Miss Mary Jane Hayes, since it opened in 1855 had 124 males and 162 females on the register of which 96 were Episcopal Church, 14 Roman Catholic, 173 Presbyterian and 3 other denominations. The other teachers were Miss J. Hagan, Miss H. Rea and Miss L. McFarlane. The Infant school children paid 1d per week which raised £21.5.0 per year. Mrs. Hayes died on 8 April 1869 and Miss M.J. Hayes was appointed in her place.

The records contain an account of a curious incident in connection with the school. In March 1870 it was reported that a Mr. Kavanagh, in giving evidence to an Inquiry into Primary Education (presumably the Powis Commission) had alleged insults to a Roman Catholic Priest, the Rev. M. Brennan, when visiting the school. The Protestant children were said to call to the Catholic children "Look at your father" and the girls to sing "I will not be a nun". The report was taken seriously by the church and the matter investigated. Signed statements refuting the allegation were published in the *Northern Star* and *Ulster Examiner,* and subsequently the Rev. Brennan stated that the incident had occurred at another school and not in Fountain Street. There is no speculation in the records as to whether this was a genuine mistake or an attempt to discredit the non-sectarian system of education strongly advocated by Scott Porter in the pamphlet *"A Plea for the United Education of the Youth of Ireland"* published by him two years earlier. He was most annoyed when the Commissioners refused to include a correction of Mr. Kavanagh's statement in their report and he obviously became suspicious of their objectivity.

It was perhaps this incident which spurred Mr. Porter to introduce a number of resolutions at the meeting of the Association of Non-Subscribing Presbyterians in June 1870 criticising the Commissioners' recommendations which he perceived would reverse the official policy for non-sectarian education introduced in 1831. In a long speech to the Association he recalled the composition of the original National board, viz. three members of the Established Church, two Roman Catholics, one orthodox Presbyterian and one Non-Subscriber. The composition was subsequently amended to become a Board of ten Protestant and ten Roman Catholic members but many members of the Board "were decidedly hostile to the principles on which the national schools had been originally founded. As a result of complaints about these inroads, Mr. Disraeli's administration had established the Commission of Inquiry in 1868. Scott Porter remarked:

"the persons who were to conduct this Inquiry had been selected with the view of carrying out the idea of concurrent endowment, so that as far as possible the schools founded and supported by the State should be no longer conducted on the original united principle, but on the denominational principle — that is to say that children should from their earliest years be kept as far as possible apart from each other and never be allowed to mix in friendly intercourse in the school-room, but be brought up under the auspices of teachers who would be selected for the special purposes of inculcating among them the theological opinions of the body to which they belong".

He said the sum and substance of the Commissioners' recommendations was:

"that in places where there is only one school united education may still continue to go on, but where there is a possibility of maintaining two schools, each numbering twenty five pupils, that these two schools shall be, one a Protestant school exclusively and the other for Roman Catholics exclusively, thus denominationalising the whole country because it is scarcely possible to fix a point in the country where two schools of twenty five each could not be started and thus the children kept separate and apart; but not only is this to be done but the books of the National Board, which contain nothing offensive to any denomination are practically to be abolished and the books published by the Christian Brothers to be introduced into the Roman Catholic schools and other descriptions of denominational books into other schools".

Scott Porter moved a number of resolutions containing the following sentiments:

"That we members of the Association of Non-Subscribing Presbyterians of Ireland feel ourselves called upon to renew, in the most emphatic terms, our declaration of attachment to the principles of united and non-sectarian education".

"We hold it indispensable that in all National Schools, and all others founded or supported by the State, the most scrupulous care should be taken to protect the consciences of those who may be in the minority in any district or who may differ from the religious opinions of the managers and teachers so as to put it out of the power of patrons or local managers of schools to make the acceptance of any particular form of religious instruction a condition of acquiring the elements of secular knowledge".

"That we regret to find that a board of commissioners who were appointed by the late government to enquire into the state of primary education in Ireland have reported, as to their opinion and advice, recommendations which would certainly and speedily have the effect of denominationalising the whole of the education given in the National Schools throughout the greater part of Ireland".

Alas for Ireland, these prescient views of Scott Porter and the Association were swamped by narrow sectarian attitudes on both sides thus deepening community division.

At the annual meeting of the congregation in 1879 it was suggested that the Fountain Street schools be dispensed with "as the time for supporting the system of non-sectarian education had long passed since that system was recognised by the National Education Board". It is not clear just what was meant by this; it seems unlikely that there was any real expectation of a change in state policy from that complained about by the Association, but more likely an expression of frustration and futility in the attempt to stem the tide.

At this time consideration was being given to the feasibility of erecting a congregational hall and one proposal was that accommodation for the schools should be incorporated in the same building. Counsel was consulted about the propriety of using the proceeds from the sale of the Fountain Street premises for a combined building but he advised against this course and the proposal was dropped. In any case the space available would not have been sufficient for a school with more than 500 pupils. Ten years later the congregation came to a firm decision to dispose of the Fountain Street schools and they were put up for auction on 15 March 1889. The reserve price of £950 was not reached at the auction but an offer at this level was received a few months later and the premises sold.

It seems, however that some elements of the congregation felt the schools should be continued and accommodation was hired in the Engineers' Hall and later in Hopeton Street. The situation at this time is described in a letter written by Mr. John Rogers (one of the Trustees) in January 1913:

"In 1889 the Fountain Street property was sold and the proceeds invested in 3½% India Stock. The interest was applied to its successor, the Hopeton Street School — that building being hired at a rent. The original manager was the Rev. A. Gordon followed by Mrs. Riddell and now the Rev. H.J. Rossington".

He appealed in his letter to the congregation for assistance to liquidate a debt of £33.1.5 and said that when the new schools in Malvern Street were erected they would be self-supporting.

A note in the annual report for 1912 about the schools includes:

"Through the generosity of the Misses Riddel, a new site for the schools has been purchased in Malvern Street, to which the Hopeton Street Schools will be removed. They have also contributed a further sum, which, with government grant will build and equip the new Schools".

In the report for 1914 it is stated:

"The completion of the new building was marked by its formal

110

opening by Miss Riddel on Friday, October 30, when there was a good attendance of persons interested in the work of the school. On November 2 the new premises were used for the first time for scholastic purposes. Since then the increased number of scholars on the roll has amply demonstrated the need of such extended accommodation".

In July 1916 the general committee approved the appointment of Messes. W.T. Hamilton, T. McErvel and Dr. M. Brice Smyth as Trustess of the Malvern Street School. In 1929 a meeting of Trustees of the school included Mr. Bowman Malcolm, Dr. Brice Smyth, Mr. T. McErvel, the Rev. R.N. Cross and Mr. J.H. Gilliland, when the business was to consider disposal of the Trust funds. The school had been transferred to the Local Education Authority on 1 April 1926. In subsequent years representatives of the congregation were elected to the Hemsworth Square Schools Committee. The Malvern Street school continues as the Riddel Memorial School and the present minister of the congregation the Rev. D.G. Banham is secretary of its management committee.

Church Interior from Pulpit   Photo: Philip McConnell

CHAPTER 8   THE CHURCH IN THE COMMUNITY

The minutes are primarily a record of the business affairs of the congregation and only incidentally refer to external events but these occasional references help to indicate the views and sympathies of the congregation at different times. Comments in calendars and annual reports are more revealing for recent times. In the earlier books there are frequent references to the "Charity Sermon" which appears to have been a major event in the church year at which a special collection was taken for the Poorhouse or school in earlier years, and later for the House of Industry and hospitals and other charities. In 1764 it was to be preached on 19 August, notice being given in Joy's paper the Friday before. In 1775 Mr. Crombie was advised to give notice of the charity sermon in the *Newsletter* and in 1778 it was to be preached on the second Sunday in August and poor boys appointed the Sunday before.

It appears that at that time a united service was held in the First House for all the congregations in the town for in 1801 Dr. Bruce reported to the committee having received a deputation from the Poorhouse committee to enquire whether this committee would approve a charity sermon being preached in each congregation in the town at the same time instead of only in one. The committee agreed to this proposal.   However in 1831 the Rev. W. Bruce informed the committee that a deputation from the Hospital committee had called on him to say that they had asked Dr. Cooke to preach their annual charity sermon and while he agreed, his committee in May Street had refused permission on account of their own debt and their promise to hold a special collection towards the building of Hilltown church, so the deputation requested the Rev. Bruce to preach the hospital charity sermon instead. The committee deprecated the decision of the May Street committee in refusing to hold the sermon in May Street for an important charity and expressed the view that new congregations should take their place in rotation. They appointed a deputation to meet the committees of the different charities and obtained agreement that charity sermons in the regular manner in which they are at present preached shall be continued in the respective congregations but other houses shall have a collection taken for the benefit of the charity on the same day.

It was apparently customary to invite special collectors for the charity sermon, for example the Rev. Bristow, Vicar of Belfast, was a collector in 1794, and in 1814 the collectors were the Marquis of Donegall, Lord Massareene, R.J. Kerr, Thos Verner, Fred Whittle and Rob Herdman. The amount of the collection is recorded on a few occasions; in 1827 it amounted to £210.13.11 (probably equivalent to about £5,000 in present-day currency) but in 1832 had declined to £63 — still a very considerable sum. By the twentieth century the current practice of taking a special monthly collection for some charity had been established.

Occasionally the committee refused requests for special collections; for example in 1825 a Mr. McMinn requested a special collection towards the erection of a presbyterian church in Donaghadee. The committee decided against such a request in principle but advised Mr. McMinn that he would be facilitated in making approaches to individual members of the congregation. Again in 1832 the Journeyman coopers of Belfast requested a special collection to enable them to emigrate but this was turned down. A request from Mountpottinger Unitarian Church in 1896 for a collection to reduce their debt was also turned down but the committee wished their cause success. In 1902 Mountpottinger made a different approach; they asked for, and were granted the use of First House for a musical performance at which they would take a special collection. Afterwards the minister reported to the committee the "scandalous conduct" of the Mountpottinger collectors in taking the collection as people entered the church demanding silver and refusing admission to those who only offered copper.

However the principle was not strictly adhered to for in 1880 a special collection was taken towards the building of a church in Newport U.S.A. to commemorate the 100th anniversary of Dr. Channing's birth and again in 1904 one was taken for the York Street congregation, the committee first having urged the York Street congregation to consider carefully whether they should not move to one of the suburbs "now that the population of Belfast was moving away from the centre". In 1939 the Rev. Herbert Barnes was invited to preach and a special collection was taken towards his new Church of Divine Unity in Newcastle-upon-Tyne.

A number of unusual causes mentioned as the objects of special collections from time to time includes: the Islands and Highlands of Scotland in 1831; the Duchess of Marlborough's Fund for "Relief of Distress in the West of Ireland" in 1880; the inhabitants of Paris who suffered from the late siege in 1871; the Liberal

Reformed Churches of France in 1889; the Pennsylvania Disaster Fund in 1889; the Non-conforming Sects of Russia in 1892 (when a Russian minister, Mr. Prelooker, was invited to preach in Rosemary Street); the Starving Children of Europe Fund in 1919; and on several occasions for the Rev. Margaret Barr's project in the Khasi Hills in India.

The use of the church was also granted to other bodies from time to time. As well as the famous occasions when it was granted to Wesley in 1789, to the Rev. Bristow in 1774 and the Rev. E. May in 1811 and 1814.; it was also granted to the Society of Friends in 1800, to the Remonstrant Presbytery of Bangor and the Remonstrant Synod of Ulster in 1830, and to the Unitarian Society and the Unitarian Men's League on numerous occasions. It was also agreed in principle to grant it to the No. 3 District of Belfast L.O.L for a service in 1951 though in the event they found it necessary to use a larger building. In 1954 it was granted to the Masonic Body for the Foundation Stone Laying Ceremony for their new Temple.

Part of church and hall c. 1890   *Photo: R. Welch*

It was customary for the church to be draped in mourning on the death of a minister or other prominent person, and always for the monarch, the last occasion being for Edward VII in 1910. On 26 August 1821 a special meeting of the committee was called to consider the propriety of putting the pulpit in mourning in consequence of the decease of her late Majesty, but it was agreed it would be inexpedient to do so and they thus indicated their disapproval of Queen Caroline. In 1827 due respects were paid to H.R.H. the Duke of York.

The congregation's contacts with the City authorities were not numerous but they are interesting. In 1864 it was decided to make no comment on the proposed changes to Hercules Street (subsequently converted to Royal Avenue). Apparently a Bill was being promoted in 1892 for a Central Railway Station in Belfast which involved a tunnel under Rosemary Street and partly under the front wall of the Central Hall. Mr. B. Malcolm reported having examined the plans and while he thought it unlikely that the work would affect the building he advised the committee to dissent from the Bill to protect their interests.

Traffic problems are not a new phenomenon for in 1872 the secretary was requested, in conjunction with the secretaries of the other two congregations, to have proper arrangements made for the arrival and departure of vehicles coming to and from the three places of worship. George Benn (8) recalls that Mrs. Ballantine and her sister Mollie Cairns came to services in the First Church in a sedan chair — perhaps the sedan chairs and carriages got in each other's way. Representations were made to the Police authorities in 1890 and again in 1904 about the closing hour for public houses coinciding with the time for evening service, this leading to a nuisance from inebriated characters in the steet when the congregation was coming to church. There was also a request to the police in 1916 to prevent newsboys selling papers in front of the church as the congregation were leaving after service, and in 1913 to disperse loafers who congregated around the entrance to the Central Hall.

In 1924 a concerted effort was made to persuade the city authorities to pave Rosemary Street with wooden blocks to reduce the noise from vehicles. It appears that the City Council was willing to bear the cost of paving the street opposite the church but would only undertake the work if other householders in the street would agree to bear the cost of paving the street opposite their premises. A similar problem had arisen just over one hundred years earlier — in 1822 — when the committee took up with the Police Committee the matter of the bad state of the pavements in Rosemary Street. At that time two members of the church committee, Messrs Black and Boyd, were deputed to measure Rosemary Street and each tenement to ascertain the cost of renewing the footpaths. They reported that the street was 350 yards long and that the cost of flagging would be 7/-d. per yard. It was then agreed to join with the Third Congregation to secure the co-operation of the inhabitants in having the work carried out, the Police Committee having agreed to bear the cost of paving opposite the churches if other inhabitants would engage to flag the footpaths opposite their own premises.

There were also long-drawn-out negotiations about the cost of water supply. The church first obtained town water supply in 1870 "enabling the ugly water barrels to be dispensed with". When the new organ was installed in 1906 the bellows were water driven. At first the Water Commissioners made a nominal charge for the supply of £1 per year but in 1911 gave notice that the water would be metered and the usual charge applied. It was estimated that over 1 million gallons would be required per year costing £38, so strong representations were made for a reduced charge but with, apparently, little effect. Apart from cost, a drought in several years (1911 and 1921) reduced the supply so much that the musical contribution to services had to be curtailed. The problem was solved eventually by the installation of an electrically driven blower, but not until 1933.

The development of the telephone service is referred to in one or two allusions; in 1893 there was a complaint that the roof of the Central Hall had been damaged by the National Telephone Company. In 1912 a proposal to install a telephone in the Hall was deferred as the National Company was about to be taken over by the Post Office. A phone was eventually installed in the Hall in 1921 and in the manse in 1923.

During the First World War a resolution from the Temperance Committee of the Non-Subscribing Church urging the government to prohibit the manufacture of intoxicating liquor for the duration of the war and six months afterwards was considered by the congregation. They obviously thought this was a little extreme and substituted an amendment to support any measures taken by the government to control the supply of drink. In 1923 the committee agreed to support a deputation being organised by Dr. Corkey to meet the Minister of Home Affairs to urge him to secure better enforcement of the law relating to gambling.

The First Church also had contacts with the United States with which friendly feeling existed; indeed at the end of the eighteenth century the United Irishmen, in which members were strongly represented, openly expressed approval of American Independence. In the seventeenth century some members had fled to America to escape episcopal domination and others had emigrated later to seek opportunities for a better living. In 1881 a letter of condolence was sent to Mrs. Garfield on the death of President Garfield and in 1930 a message was sent to the American Unitarian body on the death of ex-President Taft.

When the American Red Cross requested the use of the Central Hall in the summer of 1918 for the duration of the war and for one year afterwards it was agreed to seek alternative accommodation for congregational use so that it could be made available. However this proposal seems to have fallen through when the war ended a few weeks later. In 1925 the Rev. H.J. Rossington attended the centenary celebrations of the American Unitarians and four American ministers, Dr. G.R. Dodson of St. Louis, F.M. Eliot of St. Paul, Dr. F.R. Griffin of Philadelphia and Dr. S.B. Snow of Montreal, who visited First Church in return were each presented with a blackthorn stick. A special reception was arranged for the Rev. Dr. Preston Bradley of Chicago in 1927 and he became a regular visitor to Belfast in subsequent years, proudly boasting that his ancestors hailed from Ballymena.

The First Church was represented at European celebrations too; in 1879 the Rev. Alexander Gordon attended in Hungary the tercentenary celebrations of the Martyr death of Francis David described in the record as "the first Bishop of our Church in Transylvania" (Patrick Adair must have turned in his grave when that statement was made). In 1957 the Rev. Dr. H.J. McLachlan attended the Quincentenary celebrations of the Moravian Church in Czechoslavakia and lectured in the John Huss Faculty of the University of Prague.

A sad contact with a world event is recorded in April 1912 when the committee passed a resolution of sympathy with the widow and child of Thomas Andrews (jun.)

"may they, along with other precious memories they will cherish concerning him, find comfort in the thought of that heroic sense of duty which impelled him to the very last to think and act for others rather than himself".

Andrews had joined the congregation when he came to reside in

Belfast after his marriage in 1908. He led the team which designed and built the *Titanic* in which he lost his life.

It is unlikely that the congregation would ever have held a unanimous view on political questions and these seem to have been generally avoided, though such instances as did arise indicate a consistently liberal attitude to politics. Incidentally, one of the rules for the Central Hall, renewed periodically over the years, was that it should not be let to any political party for public political meetings. In the seventeenth century the congregation as such was under considerable pressure from time to time to conform to episcopal practice but, with others, it strenuously resisted. The relaxation of discriminatory legislation in the eighteenth century is recorded in Gordon's *Memorials.*

During that century members of the First Congregation participated prominently in public affairs. For example, of the 125 names of inhabitants appended to the address of loyalty to the Crown and Constitution directed to the Rt. Hon. Henry Boyle, speaker of the House of Commons in 1754, 28 (including Thomas Drennan) are found in the records of the congregation. In 1775 the humble Address and Petition to George III deploring the decline in trade as a result of the war in America, bore 247 names, 49 of whom (including James Crombie) are found in the congregation's records. At this period there was no complete list of members; the names available are of stipend payers or seat holders and are generally heads of families. When comparing lists of names it is common to find people of the same surname but different christian names. Such people cannot be assumed to be members though in many instances they were members of families belonging to the congregation. So the figures given in these paragraphs tend to underestimate the involvement of members.

Members were also prominent in the Volunteer forces formed to repel the threat of invasion when the army was engaged in America. Samuel McTier presided over a meeting of the Belfast Battalion on 28 August 1780 which confirmed that the standing army was subject to parliament and also called for relaxation of restrictions on trade. This meeting also agreed to form a Committee of correspondence to contact other Volunteer corps and coordinate their views. Thomas Sinclaire presided over the meeting of Belfast Volunteers called on 7 March 1782 to commend the Dungannon resolutions to the inhabitants of Belfast, and 15 of the 27 names on the letter of invitation to this meeting occur in the congregational records. The original membership of the Northern

Whig Club formed by Dr. Haliday in 1790, contained 14 Belfast residents, 9 of whom appear in the church records.

The National Convention of Volunteers which met in Dublin in 1783 was inspired by the Dungannon resolutions but it failed to secure the desired Parliamentary Reform. Dr. Drennan, under the pen name Orellana (Lawless 22) vigorously took up this cause and a few quotations from his letters illustrate the influence of his liberal religion on the attitude to political matters:

"The alliance between church and state has preserved and sanctified the abuses of both; and the same dogmatical spirit, which established for all future generations a certain system of religious belief, has transferred to our civil constitution an equal authority over the minds of men; the same reluctance to examine the grounds of our political faith, and the measures of submission to what has a century or two for its support".

"On two commands hang all the law and the prophets; and the principles of policy are not perhaps more numerous or more complex than those of religion".

"I call upon the people of Ireland, in the name of Him, the Great Philanthropist, of Him who in the torments of crucifixion sighed out his last breath for the welfare of his enemies, I call upon you Churchmen, Presbyterians and Catholics, to embrace each other in the mild spirit of Christianity and unite as a sacred compact in the cause of your sinking country".

Drennan was one of the founders of the United Irishmen, a movement which was supported by many other members of the congregation. A letter issued in January 1792 contained this sentiment:

"We anxiously wish to see the day when every Irishman shall be a citizen — when Catholics and Protestants equally interested in their country's welfare, possessing equal freedom and equal privileges, shall be cordially united, and shall learn to look upon each other as brothers, the children of the same God, the natives of the same land — and when the only strife amongst them shall be — who shall serve their country best".

Sixteen of the fifty three names appended to this letter appear in the records of the congregation.

The meeting of inhabitants called by this letter on 28 January 1792 could not be accommodated in the Town-house and so adjourned to the new meeting house. This was probably the Second House which had been rebuilt in 1789 rather than the First. The meeting was presided over by the Rev. Sinclair

Kelburn (minister of the Third Congregation) and five of the eleven speakers as recorded by Lawless were members of the First Congregation. Mr. John Holmes proposed the resolution which read:

"We therefore pray, that the legislature may be pleased to repeal, (from time to time, and as speedily as the circumstances of the country, and the general welfare of the whole kingdom will permit) all penal and restrictive statutes at present in existence against the Roman Catholics of Ireland: and that they may thus be restored to the rank and consequence of citizens in every particular".

The debate was not about whether Catholics should be emancipated; apparently all were in favour of this, but whether it should be done at once or gradually. Eventually an amendment to expunge the words in brackets above was carried by a majority and immediate emancipation advocated.

Dr. Bruce was one of those who opposed the amendment and his view that emancipation should be gradual is further confirmed by an entry in Wolfe Tone's diary following his visit to Belfast in October 1791 quoted by Mary McNeill (23):

"A furious battle, which lasted two hours, on the Catholic question, teized with the liberality of the people agreeing in principle but doubting as to the expediency. Bruce, an intolerant high priest . . . His ideas are 1st Danger to true religion inasmuch as the Roman Catholics would, if emancipated establish an inquisition. 2nd. Danger to property by reviving the Court of Claims and admitting any evidence to substantiate Catholic ideas. 3rd Danger generally of throwing power into their hands incapable of enjoying or extending liberty . . . Almost all the company of his opinion except P.P. (Russell) who made desperate battle".

This debate, on whether emancipation should be immediate or gradual, was pursued at various meetings during 1792 and early 1793 and was accompanied by civil unrest which led to an investigation by a House of Lord Committee whose report contained the following:

"The conduct of the French is shamefully extolled, and recommened to the public view, as an example for imitation; hopes and expectations have been held up of their assistance by a descent upon this kingdom, and prayers have been offered up at Belfast, from the pulpit, for the success of their arms, in the presence of military associations, which have been newly levied and arrayed in that town".

This was promptly dealt with by the dissenting ministers who met on 11 March and issued the following declaration:

"Having seen in the report of the Lords Committee dated 7th March 1793, the following words, viz., 'Prayers have been offered up at Belfast, from the pulpit, for the success of their arms — meaning the arms of the French — in the presence of military associations etc.' We, whose names are annexed, stated ministers of distinct Protestant Dissenting Congregations in the town of Belfast, do hereby declare, each of us for himself, that the information given to their Lordships of the Committee, upon this subject is, as far as concerns us, totally groundless".

The names appended to this were James Bryson, P. Vance and Will Bruce D.D. Notes to the same effect were later issued by Sinclair Kelburn and W. Carmichael.

The situation was becoming tense; the ideals of the French Revolution were advocated by United Irishmen in Belfast and its success warmly welcomed. Some militant voices were calling for more active measures than meetings and resolutions. As the support for more militant action gathered strength in the country over the next few years members of the congregation withdrew their support culminating in the message of loyalty adopted by the congregation on 28 June 1798 which contained:

"We further solemnly declare our abhorence of all foreign interference in the affairs of this Kingdom: of the present atrocious insurrection; and of all secret Cabals and Privy conspiracies to subvert or new model the Constitution without the joint consent of King, Lords and Commons in Parliament".

Lord Castlereagh's reply to this address contains:

"His excellency receives with pleasure the declaration of loyalty to our gracious Sovereign and of abhorrence of the present unprovoked and atrocious Rebellion which are contained in the address".

The movement for moderation in the congregation at that time was led by the Rev. Dr. Bruce. He had joined the Volunteers as a private when minister in Lisburn from 1779-82 and is said to have preached in his uniform on 22 July 1781. He attended the National Convention in the Rotunda in Dublin in 1783 as a delegate for Carrickfergus and moved the resolution that voting at parliamentary elections should be by ballot but this resolution was not carried.

His politics were described by Classon Porter in an article in the *Northern Whig* of 20 May 1885 as "Those of the old Whig school".

"He was an advocate for the gradual, as distinguished from the immediate, emancipation of Roman Catholics and with respect to the Society of United Irishmen, which was beginning to support the Constitutional Volunteers, Dr. Bruce published in the newspaper of the day a series of articles in which the test employed by that body was strongly condemned. To these strictures, as they appeared in the newspaper, replies were published through the same channel by Dr. Drennan of Belfast, the poet and patriot".

"In 1794 he preached in his meeting house a series of discourses on the Christian evidence in opposition to the infidel publications with which the country was deluged after the French Revolution. These discourses were largely attended and much admired. The Vicar of Belfast of those days, (the Rev. William Bristow), in order to give his people and himself an opportunity of hearing them, so arranged the services in the parish church on every Sunday of their delivery as to allow his hearers at the close of these services to be in time to attend the lectures by Dr. Bruce".

This difference of opinion between Bruce and Drennan does not seem to have caused any deep schism in the congregation the majority of whom appear to have shared Bruce's desire for a gradual transfer of political power to the Catholic's as well as for other measures to widen democracy and improve trade. In his letter of resignation in 1831 Dr. Bruce commented on the general state of the country during his ministry. He said:

"It was a period including the most awful changes in our eventful times and will be distinguished in the annals of the world for the frequency and magnitude of its political revolutions and civil convulsions, civil fueds and theological antipathy, yet this congregation maintained unblemished its high character for just principles of civil and religious liberty, internal peace and universal charity indebited no doubt in a great measure to the wisdom of its committee".

The desire for moderation was exhibited again in 1831 when the newly-formed Remonstrant Synod consulted the First Church about the terms of a proposed address to Lord Anglesey, the Lord Lieutenant. The committee advised that the address should express our attachment to the present government and our adherence to the connection with Great Britain and the principles of the British Constitution and civil and religious liberty "avoiding all irritating topics or party politics". No indication is given of what irritating topics or party politics might have been raised.

From such evidence as is available in the records over the years it can be inferred that in the nineteenth and twentieth centuries the consensus of opinion within the congregation would have favoured a local legislature and administration participated in by all sections of the community but retaining the connection with Great Britain. No comment of any kind is recorded on the division of Ireland in 1921, but it is likely that the majority, while respecting the decision of the Free State to withdraw from the United Kingdom, regretted that decision.

In October 1938 the congregation sent the following telegram to Neville Chamberlain:—

"We the members of the First Presbyterian (non-subscribing) Church, Belfast desire to extend our heartfelt thanks to you for your great services in the cause of peace. Your close connection with our household of faith is a source of pride to us all, and we feel that your actions during the trying days that have passed have been in full accord with the principle of practical Christianity for which this Church and the body to which it belongs has always taken its stand".

In 1940 a message of congratulation was sent to Mr. J.M. Andrews on his appointment as Prime Minister of Northern Ireland and in 1946 an invitation was issued to Mr. Chuter Ede, Home Secretary, to speak in the First Church when visiting Northern Ireland — in the event he was unable to find time for this. The Rev. Dr. McLachlan was Regional Officer for the United Nations Association for some years and this typified the consensus in the congregation that differences between nations and between peoples should be settled by negotiation and not by force.

The same spirit prevailed when violence erupted between the communities in Northern Ireland in the late sixties. The Rev. Wigmore-Beddoes devoted the proceeds from his booklet Preaching to a Riot to P.A.C.E. A group from the congregation travelled by bus to Drogheda to support the Peace Rally and Mr. Banham initiated a series of joint meetings between the downtown congregations. Individual members acted where and when possible to heal community divisions. In the political arena the consensus would have desired peaceful negotiation to reveal and settle grievances both real and imaginary, and to establish a liberal community in which both traditions could exist, each recognising the right of the other to hold different views. But so far this has proved impossible, each community suspects the other of a desire to dominate and impose a regime alien to its philosophy.

As Dr. Drennan pointed out two centuries ago the rigid attitudes which exist in religion in Ireland extend into the field of politics and many feel that a resolution of religious differences would pave the way for a solution of political problems. There has been much talk about ecumenism in the past decade and some useful, though limited progress has been made by the main denominations in the attempt to resolve the problems of division. But there still lingers on in most denominations vestiges of the seventeenth century attitude that they possess the truth and that those who hold different views are in error; and this attitude often renders co-operation difficult if not impossible. It is hardly to be supposed that any one of the existing denominations will succeed in persuading all the others to accept its doctrine and practice; nor is it conceivable that the leaders of the various denominations would engage in trading beliefs and practices in order to produce a set which could be agreed by all. The most likely result of such efforts would be statements couched in language so vague and ambiguous that none need object to them.

A much more honest and healthy attitude would be a frank admission that men may reach different conclusions and hold different beliefs, coupled with a firm resolve to respect and defend the right of individuals to think for themselves. If the different denominations could boldly take this step in the sphere of religion it would be easier for political parties to recognise differences in political aims and to learn to resolve differences free from the violent passions generated by narrow religious conviction.

Interior of Church 1886

CHAPTER 9
THE THEOLOGICAL STANCE OF THE CONGREGATION

At the beginning of the seventeenth century Papacy, Protestant Episcopacy and Presbyterianism were the main contenders for supremacy, each with the aim of imposing its system of church government and beliefs on all others. Only the Independents aimed at freedom for themselves and others to adopt whatever system seemed best to them. Speaking of the attitude of the various religious factions in Ireland at that time Ramsay Colles (9) says:

"The exponents of each creed set forth its dogmas in stern array, to be accepted without demur. Each church believed that it alone had received the divine injunction to propagate the truth even at the point of the sword. The very idea of religious toleration was itself intolerable".

The "Necessary Representation" drawn up by the Presbytery in Belfast on 15 February 1649 to the English Parliament protested against the execution of the King and Parliament's repudiation of the covenant but, significantly, also against Parliament's toleration of other forms of religion:

"What of late have been, and now are insolent and presumptious practices of the Sectaries in England. . . since they have with a high hand despised the oath in breaking the covenant . . . and likewise labour to establish by laws an universal toleration of all religions which is an innovation overturning the unity of religion and so directly repugnant to the word of God. . . ."

Anthony Shaw was no doubt one of the authors of this document and, since a copy was found among Patrick Adair's papers when he was arrested in 1653, he too shared this sentiment as indeed is obvious from the whole tenor of his narrative.

They received an interesting and scathing reply to the Representation from John Milton, the recently appointed Latin Secretary to Cromwell's Council. He asserted that the Council had endeavoured to extirpate papacy and prelacy and heresy and schism by all effectual and proper means:

"but these divines might know that to extirpate all those things can be no work of the civil sword, but of the spiritual which is the word of God . . . and by the power of truth, not of persecution subduing these authors of heretical opinions . . . ."

Milton, though nominally a member of the Church of England

was by no means orthodox in his theology. He had produced a treatise in 1642 arguing against prelacy and favouring a presbyterian form of church government.

However he changed his view a few years later as described by Hutchinson (24):

"It would not be long before Milton's passing preference for presbyterianism would be abandoned when he saw the intolerance and rigid discipline of the Westminster Assembly of Divines".

After the Restoration (when Milton lost his government appointment and was lucky to escape more severe censure) he gave an indication of his theology in *Paradise Lost* and *De Doctrina* in which he expressed what were essentially Arian views. Hutchinson sums up Milton's attitudes thus:

"He claimed and exercised the right to think for himself, to form his own political judgements, and to interpret the scripture in his own way with singularly little regard for tradition or authority".

Although in subsequent centuries members of the First Church were to come to accept much of Milton's philosophy it is unlikely that they did so in his time.

There is little on record of the Rev. William Keyes's opinions. He was apparently flexible to some degree since, with Richardson, he was willing, on Monk's advice to amend the Presbytery's address to Charles II by deleting references to prelacy and the covenant. However he refused to yield to episcopalian pressure to conform in 1661 and subsequently spent two years in Galway gaol.

According to Reid (4) McBride played a leading part in the struggle for toleration for dissenters in the last decade of the seventeenth century. He engaged in exchanges with Bishops Pullen and Edward Synge. In the course of one of his pamphlets he said of dissenters:

"They believe the necessity of a standing Gospel ministry in the Church, to whose direct authority they submit themselves, not by an implicit faith, but by a judgment of discretion".

This sentiment might be regarded as heralding the beginnings of the more flexible attitudes soon to appear in the First Church. McBride certainly exhibited a degree of integrity characteristic of subsequent ministers when his refusal to take the Oath of Abjuration was said to be based on the fact that he could not personally know that the Pretender was not James's son.

The Rev. Samuel Haliday was noted mainly for his refusal to subscribe the Westminster Confession of Faith at his installation in 1719. When invited by the Moderator of the General Synod of Ulster on 20 June 1721 to reaffirm his adherence to the Confession, Haliday said:

"My refusal to declare my adherence to the assent I gave to the Westminster Confession of Faith at an earlier date, does not proceed from my disbelief of the important truths contained in it, the contrary of which I have oft by word and writing declared, but my scruples are against the submitting to human tests of Divine truths, especially in a great number of the extra essential points without the knowledge and belief of which man may be entitled to the favours of God and hopes of eternal life . . ." (Records of General Synod of Ulster 25).

Haliday declined to give reasons for his scruples "to avoid heat and altercation". His stand brought the subscription controversy to a head at this time leading to the establishment of the non-subscribing Presbytery of Antrim in 1725. According to Alex. Gordon "the doctrine of the Trinity has never been preached among us since Drennan lifted up his gentle voice in 1736" so apparently the theological views of the congregation underwent a considerable evolution in the first half of the eighteenth century.

Crombie's views on church consecration are published in an article included as an appendix to Micaiah Twogood's *A Dissent from the Church of England fully justified"* by Alex. Wilkinson, Newry 1816. Crombie had been told that the Rev. W. Bristow had cast aspersions on the dissenters of Belfast at the consecration of St. Anne's. His charity of outlook is manifest in the way he dismisses the rumour:

"I am apt to believe they must be founded on a misapprehension of the preacher's words. For I cannot allow myself to think that he would have used the expressions that might have the least tendency to disturb that perfect harmony which has so long subsisted between the members of the Established Church and the Protestant Dissenters of Belfast" (A marginal note in the copy of the book in the congregational library recalls that the Rev. Bristow had been given the use of the meeting house in 1774-7).

He goes on to deal with the myths and superstitions surrounding the rite of dedication referring particularly to the Folio edition printed by Grierson in 1760 of the *Directory for the Consecration of Churches and Chapels according to the use of the*

Church of Ireland. Based on the text "The hour cometh, saith he, and now is, when the true worshippers shall worship the Father in spirit and in truth, for the Father seeketh such to worship him" Crombie asserts:

"Here is a plain declaration that under the gospel, the worship of God was to derive its value, not from the place of the worshipper, but from the temper of his mind. . . Jesus represented the Father of the Universe as everywhere present, and as ready to hear any worshipper that worships him in spirit and in truth; he fixed no limitations as to place or situation".

It is interesting to compare this view with that expressed by Milton a century earlier in *De Doctrina* of which Hutchinson says "He scouts the notion of consecrated buildings, for holiness is not in place at all".

The Rev. Dr. Bruce, who succeeded Crombie, was quite explicit about his Unitarian theology. In the Epistle Dedicatory to his *Sermons on the Study of the Bible* published by J. Hodgson, Belfast 1826 he says:

"The Antitrinitarian and Arminian doctrines recommended in these sermons are the same that were formerly inculcated by those eminent Ministers, Haliday and my grandfather, Drennan and Brown, Mackay and Crombie and lastly by myself and my dear son, neither shackled by subscriptions, nor guided by formularies. Of the principles of older ministers, Kirkpatrick, McBride and Adair, all distinguished men in their day, I am not competent to speak with precision".

The essence of Bruce's theology can be gleaned from a quotation from one of the sermons in this volume:

"If then, you are in doubt, whether any doctrine be necessary to salvation try it by this test, look for it in the gospels; and if you do not find it plainly declared in them all, you may safely conclude that it is not essential to the plan of redemption . . . Scripture abounds with truths, conducive to edification, able to 'convert the soul, rejoice the heart and enlighten the mind' but I speak at present only of such as are essential to salvation and declared to be so by our Lord. These are faith and repentance, love to God and love to men . . . That they are sufficient is repeatedly declared by Christ".

The Biblical scholar, John Scott Porter, who succeeded the Bruces also held Unitarian views expounded in detail in his controversy with the Rev. Daniel Bagot M.A., held in the First Church in 1834 and subsequently published under *Report of Discussion on the Unitarian Controversy* by Simms & McIntyre, Belfast 1834, and in his *Twelve Lectures in illustration and defence of Christian Unitarianism* Simms & McIntyre 1841.

At the installation of Alexander Gordon in 1877 the chairman, Mr. E.J. Harland in the course of his speech said:

"I think I may venture to say that Belfast is looked upon as a centre, if not the centre, of Christian Unitarianism in the United Kingdom. Although we bear the name of the 'First Presbyterian Congregation' it is more strictly applicable to us in a chronological sense; as something like 235 years ago Scotch Presbyterianism was introduced into this neighbourhood, perhaps the only one where any religious toleration whatever was to be found extended to its ministers. At that time, and for near a hundred years subsequently, the great and good men who adorned the ranks of the predecessors of our present pastor appear to have been devoted almost exclusively to securing religious liberty, rather than to declamation upon any delicate point of theology".

At the same function the Rev. Alexander Gordon referred to his mission as including: "the expounding of Unitarian Christianity to this congregation and this neighbourhood". However, in reply, the Rev. J. Scott Porter pointed out:

"Unitarianism is certainly the prevailing sentiment in our Church, but I wish to say upon this public occasion . . . that ours is not a Unitarian Church. Ours is a Church free in point of theology; free to accept Unitarianism if we like it; free to reject it if we find a better way. We are Non-subscribing Presbyterians".

In a letter to Gordon accompanying a purse towards his expenses in attending the Francis Dávid tercentenary in Hungary in 1879 the committee said "you will be able to afford our brethren in the far east an assurance of our deep sympathy with them in upholding so steadily and continuously, as they have done for so many centuries, the pure and practical religion of the good and great Unitarian martyr".

At this time the Press frequently referred to the congregation as Unitarian and indeed on its own notepaper and other publications the term "Unitarian" was often placed in brackets after First Presbyterian. On several occasions at the end of the nineteenth and in the early twentieth centuries a proposal to adopt the name Unitarian was moved in committee but always rejected. Scott Porter's description was the one that prevailed and the sentiments it embodies were voiced by Mr. James Carr in 1895 at the installation of the Rev. Douglas Walmsley:

"What was their mission (speaking of the group of liberal churches). . . one branch of the mission, and not an unimportant branch, was to diffuse among the members of other Churches that broad spirit of liberality, charity and tolerance which came very near the corner stone of their own. Who knew but the time might yet come when the diffusion of that spirit might break down the barriers that divided the creed-bound Churches all over the world and gradually work such a revolution in religious thought that thereafter the tendings of all religious forces would be centripetal and not centrifugal".

Other voices, too, were raised for universality as opposed to denominationalism in religion. At the installation of the Rev. R. Nicol Cross in 1928, the Rev. R.W. Seaver M.A., B.D., of St. John's, Malone, is reported to have suggested that the different churches should drop their theology and exalt their religion and expressed the hope that the day would come when there would be one great Church in Belfast. At the same function the Rev. Dr. Frazer-Hurst of Elmwood said that no individual or church possessed a monopoly of truth and it was only as they had the same spirit of charity and brotherliness that they could do anything worthwhile. These sentiments would be warmly welcomed by members of the congregation for whom the Rev. Dr. R.W. Wilde crystallised their theological outlook when he said in *Three Hundred Years of Worship, Work and Witness* in 1944:

"Who can define with any exactitude the precise nature and being of Him who holdeth Orion and Pliades in the hollow of his hand, before Whom the nations are but a drop in a bucket? Such questions are best approached with an attitude of reverent agnosticism".

Denominationalism was not the only problem which occupied the congregation in the twentieth century but the growth of so-called secularism received increasing attention. But it was not something to be suppressed or even ignored but rather something to be understood and integrated into a satisfactory philosophy of life. An extract from the annual report for 1928 reads:

"We are still in a period of wide unsettlement among thinking people, many of whom find that religion, if it is to survive as a faith for them, must be rebuilt on foundations not merely of tradition and authority, but of reason and experience and that the most ancient doctrines must be adjusted so as to be in harmony with the new world of knowledge created mainly by science".

A note in the calendar for November 1930 in connection with a series of special sermon subjects on Modern Problems of Thought and Life deals with current attitudes to religion:

"In certain quarters there is open and convinced attack e.g. Mr. Bertrand Russell in England, and notably also in Russia where atheism and irreligion are erected into a system of government. But much more widespread are doubt and scepticism in regard to religion and all its doctrines and claims into which multitudes have drifted of thought themselves. Many of them are good sincere people who would fain believe if they could, and pulpit denunciation is not the remedy. The hope of the recovery or confirmation of religious faith lies in sympathetic understanding and serious reasoning and this is the method we shall adopt in the desire to be helpful to those who are in real difficulty about religion".

Religious bigotry, too, was vigorously condemned as a cancer in society. A note in the calendar for February 1934 dealing with a series of sermons on "Great Persecutions" contains:

"It is hard for us to-day to realise that the early church communities were hated as criminal institutions, but such is the common attitude of popular bigotry and superstition, and it affords a warning against intolerance and the spirit that condemns without serious effort to understand".

A "Message for the New Year" in the calendar for January 1961 contained the following revealing and prophetic passage:

"One may be pardoned for thinking that the controversies over church aims and rights and the theological doctrines that go on around us to-day are a kind of fiddling while Rome burns. The clash of human opinion and the wrath of Sectaries about words and doctrine and meanings are endless. It has gone on for centuries. It has filled millions of printed pages and consumed millions of hours of thought. The dusty shelves of a thousand libraries witness to its futility and the world is no better for it.

Theological strife is, however, meat and drink to a diminishing number of persons living in backwaters and up the cul-de-sacs of history, and Ulster has more than its share of these troglodytes. But the world and its future are not going to be influenced by such oddities. Like Canute they gesticulate in vain. The waters of contemporary life will eventually leave them stranded or submerge them utterly.

The pity is that they appear to command far more attention than they deserve. Allowing for the obvious "press value" of the strange and startling, it would seem wise on the part of the ordinary citizen and those who control our newspapers to give as little publicity to sectarian strife as possible.

Those elements in our society who wish to stir up trouble should be fairly and firmly subdued and one way of doing this is to discountenance their activities and ignore their pretensions.

Religion is not a matter of words and doctrines. It is primarily a disposition, a way of life. Biblical fundamentalism and intolerant literalism are manifestly anti-religious in the deepest sense of the word. They are also dangerous in the context of the tensions of our time. Bible thumping is no more religious than drum beating".

A note on the evil of excessive Sabbatarianism in the calendar for November 1966 ends:

"The point to bear in mind is that Christianity is a religion of the spirit, not a religion of external authority. It is only as the human spirit recognises the spiritual authority of the Master and reflects his faith, hope and love in everyday life that true religion is born and can flourish, making every day sacred and regarding every human being as a child of God".

Over the three and a half centuries of its existence the congregation has evolved from a rigid Calvinist theology which sought to impose its standards on all over whom it could gain control, to a free stance in which individual members frame their own beliefs and accept responsibility for their own actions. These changes have led to misunderstandings about the congregation over the years. The name presbyterian is properly used because it adopts the democratic presbyterian form of church government though it has long since abandoned the rigid Calvinist theology frequently associated with presbyterianism, but not necessary to it. Its nearest relatives in the world of theology are the Unitarians and in the last century (and possibly also at present) most members would describe themselves as such, for present day Unitarians are essentially non-subscribers having outgrown the biblical Arianism which gave rise to the name. There is to-day, no fixed body of beliefs which all Unitarians accept, and indeed a continuous evolution of thought and expression is the prominent character-istic of Unitarian theology from the time of Bruce. But the First Church has avoided adopting the name Unitarian since others are apt to assume that such a name implies subscription to particular fixed beliefs, to the exclusion of those who cannot so subscribe.

In past centuries people holding such ideas were regarded by most religious institutions as dangerous heretics to be ostracised if not tortured or burned. It is only in very recent times that prominent members of other churches such as Bishop John Robinson or Dr. Don Cupitt considered it prudent to raise difficult theological questions publicly, and even yet scholars in the Roman Catholic Church such as Edward Shillebeecks and Hans Küng are called to account for raising such questions.

There may still be some people who require an unquestioning faith based on the authority of a church but it is evident that increasing numbers do not find this adequate and react by ignoring the churches and their doctrines altogether. Yet men know in their hearts that this universe with all its ordered content is not just a purposeless accident. Such people need to seek a reasonable explanation and the First Church seeks to meet that need.

*Rev. Dr. H. J. McLachlan M.A., B.D.,
Minister 1952 — 1967*

*Rev. D. G. Wigmore Beddoes M.A., F. R. Hist. S.
Minister 1968 — 1974*

*Rev. D. G. C. Banham T. Eng., B.D.
Minister 1975 —*

REFERENCES

1. The Constitutional History of Modern Britain since 1485
   Sir David Lindsay Keir   London 1960

2. The Origins of European Dissent
   R.I. Moore   London 1977

3. Living Faiths
   Edited by R.C. Zachner   London 1959

4. History of the Presbyterian Church in Ireland
   James S. Reid   Belfast 1867

5. Irish Unitarian Magazine Vol.1 No. IV   Belfast 1846

6. A True Narrative of the Presbyterian Church in Ireland
   Patrick Adair   Ed. Dr. W.D. Killen   Belfast 1866

7. The Scottish Covenanters and Irish Confederates
   D. Stevenson   Belfast 1981

8. History of Belfast
   George Benn   London and Belfast 1877

9. History of Ulster
   Ramsay Colles   4 Vols.   London 1920

10. Historical Notices of Old Belfast
    R.M. Young   Belfast 1896

11. Historic Memorials of the First Presbyterian Church, Belfast
    Alexander Gordon   Belfast 1887

12. The Ulster Scot. His History and Religion
    J.B. Woodburn   London 1914

13. The Town Book of Belfast
    Ed. R.M. Young   Belfast 1892

14. The Churches and Abbeys of Ireland
    B. de Breffny and G. Mott   London 1976

15. Roger Mulholland Architect of Belfast 1740—1818
    C.E.B. Brett   Belfast 1976

16. Long Shadows Cast Before
    C.E.B. Brett   London 1978

17. The Synagogue
    Isaac Levy   London 1964

18. History of the Second Congregation
    S. Shannon Millan   Belfast 1900

19. The History of the Royal Belfast Academical Institution
    John Jamieson   Belfast 1959

20. Daniel O'Connell and his World
    Dudley Edwards   London 1975

21. Vere Foster: An Irish Benefactor
    Mary McNeill   Newtown Abbot 1971

22. Belfast Politics Enlarged
    John Lawless   Belfast 1818

23. The Life and Times of Mary Ann McCracken
    Mary McNeill   Dublin 1960

24. Milton and the English Mind
    F.E. Hutchinson   London 1946

25. Records of the General Synod of Ulster
                                                    Belfast 1897

    Alexander Gordon
    H. McLachlan   Manchester 1932

APPENDIX 1: CONGREGATIONAL RECORDS

The material for this account has been obtained mainly from the following sources:
1. Minute books
2. Annual reports
3. Monthly and quarterly calendars
4. Baptismal, Marriage and Funeral Registers
5. Account book for period 1781—1859
6. Scrap book for period 1812—1877
7. Historic Memorials of the First Presbyterian Church Rosemary Street by Rev. Alexander Gordon, Belfast 1887
8. Three Hundred Years of Worship, Work and Witness by Rev. Dr. R.W. Wilde, Belfast 1944.

MINUTE BOOKS

The known congregational minute books are:

1. For period from 3. 2. 1760 till 1. 1. 1775
2.   20.8.1775 till 20.2.1785
3.   1. 4. 1781 till 10.6.1819
4.   13.6.1819 till 18.4.1841
5.   18.4.1841 till 18.4.1863 (missing)
6.   26.4.1863 till 25.5.1880
7.   27.5.1880 till 25.9.1892
8.   2.10.1892 till 14.4.1901
9.   5. 6. 1901 till 18.3.1910
10.   13.4.1910 till 16.2.1921
11.   28.2.1921 till 3. 7. 1931
12.   3. 7. 1931 till 2. 2. 1945
13.   21.1.1945 till 8. 1. 1954
14.   10.1.1954 till 4.10.1968
15.   1.11.1968 till 27.1.1980

The first fourteen of these are pre-bound books into which the minutes are written in manuscript, since 1968 they have been typed and kept in loose leaf binders to be bound later in convenient volumes.

It is not known whether there were earlier minutes of congregational bodies which have been mislaid or lost. Alexander Gordon assumed that No. 1 above was the first since it commenced with a scheme for the election of a committee to manage "along with the Session", the affairs of the congregation. It is not conclusive that this was the first committee for on two subsequent occasions in 1768 and 1790 meetings of Heads of Families were called to elect a committee to manage the affairs of the congregation, so the 1760 episode may have been only one such occasion among others the only difference being that a record of its formation exists. The 1760 scheme did, however, provide that "a book be kept in the Session-house wherein the transactions of the Committee shall be regularly entered and the minutes of every meeting signed by the Chairman" from which it may be inferred that this had not previously been the practice. If there was no committee prior to 1760 presumably the session had dealt with business relating to the congregation since it was established in 1644 but no record of its activity exists except for references in the funeral register to decisions of the joint sessions (i.e. of the First and Second Congregations) in 1716, 1721, 1723 and 1727.

The first two minute books were re-bound by the British Museum in 1908 as was also the funeral register. Book No. 1 was treated by placing fine silk on either side of the pages which it was said would prolong its life for another 300 years.

The legibility of the writing varies considerably, the first four books contain writing by a number of different hands some of which are difficult to read but most of it can be deciphered except for occasional words or phrases. Books 6 to 9 inclusive are very carefully written and as Smith and McTear were secretaries at this time it seems likely that the minutes were written by professional scriveners in their office (solicitors). Apparently draft minutes were first produced as there is a volume of draft minutes within this period in the Public Record Office. Subsequent books, though less professionally written, can be read fairly easily.

That Book No. 5 existed is confirmed by an entry in the title page of Book No. 6 which reads "last minute book commenced on 18th April 1841 and ended on 18th April 1863". It appears to have been available to Alexander Gordon in the 1880s from his comment "the placid pages of our congregational minute book, at the period of the passing of the Bill (Dissenters Chapels Act 1844) quiver with the agitation of that momentus struggle". The minutes of a committee meeting held on 4 April 1894 record that the secretary had consulted the minutes of a meeting held on 7 March 1852 and these would have been in Book No. 5. There are several references in minutes for 1914 to the need to recover minute books which had been kept by Mr. J.S. McTear (who died in 1913 while still secretary) but no details of the books in question are given.

In February 1923 a sub-committee was appointed to examine historic documents belonging to the congregation. It did not report that Book No. 5 was missing but neither did it report No. 6 missing although it must then have been so, since Mr. Rossington reported in December 1923 that minute book No. 6 had been returned by a Mr. Robinson of Messrs Fisher & Co. No explanation is given of how it had strayed from congregational custody but perhaps No. 5 strayed by the same route. After the air-raids in 1941 the minute books (along with other documents) were sent to Rademon for safe keeping. No. 1 to 4 and 6 to 11 are listed but there is no mention of No. 5 so it seems to have been missing for more than half a century.

This is unfortunate for it covered the period immediately after the Sunday school and day school were started; two important pieces of legislation the Dissenters Chapels and Marriage Acts, the opening of the Domestic Mission and the installation of the first organ in the church. It also covered the period of the famine in Ireland so there is no record of any part played by the congregation in famine relief. During this period too (1862) the Presbytery of Antrim split into two factions viz. the Presbytery of Antrim and the Northern Presbytery of Antrim. There is thus no record of the views of the First Church on the controversy but the fact that it joined the less radical Northern Presbytery of Antrim is an indication.

The minutes deal with the business affairs of the congregation recording resolutions made and, often, an indication of the arguments for and against a proposition. They seldom contain a definite record that action had been taken unless when some further problem arose in connection with it. The most complete record of action taken is in annual reports. There are very few references in the minutes to theological, moral or social issues, though sometimes attitudes can be inferred from comments and decisions recorded. The minute books are not indexed but in 1980 chronological abstracts of important matters were made. Four copies of these were typed and bound and they provide a relatively speedy means of locating particular items in the voluminous minutes.

ANNUAL REPORTS

Regular annual business meetings of the congregation appear to have commenced in 1812 and in 1818 the committee's annual report is written into the minutes. This occurred again in 1840 at the end of Book No. 4, and from the beginning of Book No. 6 in 1863 it appears to have been an established practice so it is possible that reports for each year were recorded in the missing minute book. The first printed copy of the report extant is for the year 1867—8 pasted into the scrap book. Copies exist for most years since then either in the scrap book, minute books or in bound volumes. Up until 1908 it was customary to print a draft report prior to the annual meeting and a final copy afterwards.

In 1933 when the celebration of the 150th anniversary of the church building was being discussed it was resolved to collect annual reports and monthly calendars for binding into convenient volumes. When a volume of annual reports for the years 1912—31 came to the notice of the committee in 1969 it was decided to attempt to complete the collection and in future to bind copies in decades. This resulted in the production of volumes covering the periods 1935—49; 1950—59; 1960—69 and 1970—79. However in 1979 when the library books were being sorted after restoration work following bomb damage, another bound volume covering the years 1932—51 was found, rsulting in an overlap in the collection. At this time also a collection of early reports for the years 1871—98 (with a few missing) was found and these have also been bound resulting in an almost complete set spanning a century. The annual reports contain information about congregational activities, property maintenance and repair, membership and finance. Obituaries were included from the first and baptisms and weddings since 1941.

CALENDARS

The first printed calendar was for the month of October 1926 and they continued monthly until 1974. Since the autumn of 1975 a quarterly calendar in stencilled form has been produced. Copies of most of the calendars since 1926 are pasted into the relevant minute books though some are missing. These calendars give details of services, congregational activities, baptisms, marriages and deaths. They often also contain comment on current affairs and thus provide, with annual reports, a more complete record of the congregation than is available for the earlier period before they were issued.

REGISTERS

According to Alexander Gordon the first volume of the Baptismal Register had been missing since 1790 but he cites no evidence for its existence and there is no reference to it in minute books. The second volume which began in 1756 is still in use. It is kept in the Public Record Office and entries are transferred to it from a bound duplicate book. Gordon reproduced considerable extracts from it in *Historic Memorials*. The certificate of the registration of the Meeting House for solemnising marriages is dated 15th April 1845 and the Marriage Register contains entries from 1846. The first Funeral Register in existence was begun in 1712 and much of it, too, is reproduced in *Historic Memorials*.

ACCOUNT BOOK 1781—1859

There are various account books and ledgers in the safes but the most interesting of these is the earliest covering the period 1781—1859. It commences with the list of subscribers to the Building Fund for the new meeting house; of the ladies of Belfast who subscribed for the pulpit; details of the loan obtained from Dr. Crombie and its repayment, and other building funds in 1841—9 and 1849—59 as well as annual stipend accounts.

SCRAP BOOK 1812—77

This is an unusual but valuable book into which various documents are pasted — mainly notices for the annual meeting. At first these contain lists of seat holders and members of committee; from 1861 a statement of accounts is included and from 1867 a copy of the annual report. From the dates it seems likely that this collection was commenced by the Rev. Wm. Bruce and continued by the Rev. J. Scott Porter after Bruce's death.

HISTORIC MEMORIALS

The congregation seems to have become conscious of its unique historical role in the church life of Belfast at the end of the nineteenth century. There is no record of any celebration or other notice taken of the bicentenary of the congregation in 1844 (or 1842) but because the minute book and annual reports for those years are missing it is not possible to be definite that the event went entirely unmarked. In contrast, the centenary celebration of the present meeting house in 1883 was a grand affair. The fact that the minister of the day, the Rev. Alexander Gordon, was an historian, and one of the chief historians of Belfast, Mr. George Benn, was a member of the congregation, was no doubt responsible for the interest then taken.

These centennial celebrations culminated in a large gathering in the Ulster Hall on 20 June 1883 for which the first print of 1000 tickets was insufficient. It was later described as the largest gathering of Unitarians and their friends ever to assemble in Ireland. The guest speakers at this event included the Rev. Wm. Napier, Sir James C. Lawrence, Mr. David Martineau, the Rev. Dr. A.P. Putnam and the Rev. Dr. Bryce. In connection with the celebration the *Historic Memorials of the First Presbyterian Church of Belfast* by the Rev. Alexander Gordon printed by Marcus Ward & Co. Belfast 1887 was produced. (Marcus Ward was also a member of the congregation).

The tercentenary of the founding of the congregation celebrated in 1944 in wartime conditions was also quite an occasion. It culminated with a meeting in the Grand Central Hotel on 19 June 1944 at which the guest speakers included the Very Rev. W.

M. Kennedy, retiring Moderator of the General Assembly, Sir Crawford McCullough, Lord Mayor of Belfast, the Very Rev. W.S. Kerr, Dean of Belfast, Sir D. Lindsay Keir, Vice-Chancellor of Queens University, Mr. F.J. Cole representing the Methodist Church, Mr. Geo Alexander, Chairman of the Congregational Union and the Rev. R.G. Lloyd of the Moravian Church. In connection with this event a booklet *Three Hundred Years of Worship, Work and Witness* was produced by the Rev. Dr. R.W. Wilde which included contributions from former ministers, the Rev. H.J. Rossington and the Rev. Nicol Cross, and from Mr. Albert Taylor the church organist.

APPENDIX 2: MINISTERS OF THE CONGREGATION

John Baird	1642
Anthony Shaw	1646—1649
— Read	1650—
William Keyes	1660—1673
Patrick Adair	1674—1694
John McBride	1694—1718
Dr. James Kirkpatrick (Asst.)	1706—1708
Thos. Milling (Asst.)	1714—1719
Samuel Haliday	1720—1739
Thomas Drennan	1736—1768
Andrew Millar (Asst.)	1749—1756
James Mackay	1756—1781
John Beatty (Asst.)	1768—1770
Dr. James Crombie	1770—1790
Dr. William Bruce	1790—1841
William Bruce	1812—1868
J. Scott Porter	1832—1880
Alex Gordon	1877—1890
J. Kirk Pike	1891—1894
Douglas Walmsley	1894—1906
H.J. Rossington	1907—1927
R. Nicol Cross	1928—1938
Dr. R.W. Wilde	1939—1950
Dr. H.J. McLachlan	1952—1967
D.G. Wigmore-Beddoes	1968—1974
D.G.C. Banham	1975—

APPENDIX 3: SINGING CLERKS AND ORGANISTS

Singing Clerks
(Names mentioned in records between 1771 and 1840 in chronological order).

John Cochran	Thomas Bruce
Ernest Cochran	Mr. Cordner
Mr. McVity	Mr. Pearce
Mr. Barr	Mr. Murray
Mr. Hughes	

Organists

1853 W.S. Burnett	1907 A. Davies
1864 Dr. Hobson Carroll	1910 J.T. Thompson
1888 R.S. Liddell	1912 L.C. Buckley
1889 G.F. Stewart	1913 W. Layton
1892 W.J. Crowe	1918 A. Taylor
1896 G.C. Ferguson	1950 L. James
1896 L.R. Glenton	1956 Dr. J. McCloy
1900 Miss Brogden (later Mrs. Neill)	1957 W.T. Beattie
1904 W.H. Wood	1958 G. Gibson
1905 J. Douglas	1962 Wm. McCay
1905 W.H. Wood	1978 J.W. Foster
	1979 R.A. Megraw

139

APPENDIX 4: CHURCH OFFICERS

Treasurers

1712 Thomas Lyle
1713 John Ewing
1714 John Euless
1715 William Mitchell
1716 Uchtred McDoull
1717 John McMunn
1760 John Ross
1761 John Galt Smith
1781 Robert Gordon
1790 John Holmes
1802 John Holmes Houston
1817 William Tennent
1827 Robert Callwell
1836 Robert Montgomery
1851 Wm. J.C. Allen
1869 James Carr
1874 Nicholas Oakman
1876 Wm. H. Patterson
1881 John W. Russell
1886 John Rogers
1893 James Davidson
1915 Wm. T. Hamilton
1921 Wm. Greenfield
1923 Wm. McRobert
1946 David McMurray
1953 Wm. R. Beattie
1956 Hugh McRobert
1967 Wm. R. Beattie
1971 Jack Robinson
1983 Jim Swann

Secretaries

1760 Charles Cunningham

1771 Robert Gordon

1782 Rev. Jas. Crombie

1817 John Ward
1827 Wm. Patterson
1837 Thomas Chermside
1839 George K. Smith
1886 John S. McTear
1914 Eustace Gordon
1925 James H. Gilliland
1938 William J. Tate
1941 Hugh McRobert
     A.R. McNeill
1944 Margaret E. Wood
1951 Robert Wilkinson
1954 Thomas Moore
1957 Thomas Moore
     May Megaw
1971 Thomas Moore
     Nora Trueick
1981 Thomas Moore
     Hilary Wallace

APPENDIX 5: CONGREGATIONAL TRUSTEES

J.G. Smith
John Curell
J.T. Tennent
J.G. Smith
Wm. Hartley
G.K. Smith
W.J.C. Allen
J.M. Darbishire
E.J. Harland
W.S. Boyd
F. Little
G. Andrews
B. Malcolm
R. Patterson
F.H. Rogers
A.H.R. Carr
R. McCrum

T.H. McMurray
C.J. McKisack
J. McCaw
W.C. Dobbin
J. Montgomery
W.W. Barry
D. McMurray
Wm. McRobert
R. Wilkinson
J.A. Chambers
W. Baxter
T. Moore
F. Smyth
Mrs. N. Trueick
M. Fieldhouse
Wm. McCay

APPENDIX 6: BEQUESTS

1803   John Mathers — £100
1818   Mary Hodgens — £50
1818   Miss McIlwrath — £50
1833   Wm. Tennent: Moiety of Skipper Street rent.
1841   Rev. Dr. Bruce — £50
1851   Robert Montgomery — £50
1859   Jane Whitla — £50

1861	Elizabeth McKedy — £100	1947	Miss M. Service — £100
1861	Catherine McKedy — £50	1950	W.T. Scott — £100
1861	Mary McKedy — £50	1954	C.J. McKisack — £500
1872	John Galt Smith — £100	1954	Miss E. Erskine — £100
1875	Andrew Kirk (manse) — £1258	1954	Miss Anna Fitzgerald — £200
1879	William Campbell — £100	1957	Miss E.J. Leith — £200
1882	Miss Jane Curell — £50	1957	Miss C. McFadden — £100
1884	William J.C. Allen — £100	1957	Miss M. Irvine — £250
1886	George K. Smith — £200	1958	Miss A.M. Fitzgerald — £200
1896	Sir James Musgrave — £50	1962	Miss A.F.V. McAdoo — £200
1896	William Riddel — £100	1963	Miss E.J. Erskine — £100
1901	Anne J. Campbell — £100	1963	Miss E.J. Lilburn — £50
1902	Mrs. George Benn — £100	1963	Mrs. E.C. Harvey — £200
1917	James Davidson — £250	1966	Mrs. F.J. Davidson — £150
1924	Miss C. Bruce — £100	1969	Mrs. S. Mawhinney — £150
1924	Miss E. Bruce — £100	1972	Miss A.C. Moore — £280
1924	Miss E. Riddel — £1000	1975	J.A. Campbell — £100
1926	Miss Susan Bruce — £200	1976	Miss M. Boas — £150
1928	Miss M.E. Porter — £100	1977	J.J. Bell — £1000
1934	Victor Jennings — £100	1978	Capt. McNinch — £500
1934	Miss F.M. McTear — £100	1978	Miss B. Weaver — £100
1937	Miss M.A. Gracey — £100	1979	Miss M.J. Wilson — £250
1943	Miss R. Moore — £209	1980	Miss Mary Russell — £100
1947	Miss E. Carlisle — £50	1980	Miss Dorothy Kennedy — £500

APPENDIX 7: THE CHANGING VALUE OF THE POUND

The rapid decline in the value of the pound in recent years prompts an attempt to construct a scale of values which would facilitate a comparison between sums of money quoted at various periods over this history with the present day value of the pound.

There is no recognised authoritative scale so one has been constructed using a combination of several overlapping indexes. Those used are the General Index of Retail Prices covering the period since 1956, the Interim Index of Retail Prices for the period 1948 till 1956, the Cost of Living Index 1914—1947 and a Cost of Living Index given by E.H. Phelps Brown in *A Century of Pay* covering the period 1860—1913. No reliable data have been found for earlier times.

These indexes are compiled on different bases so when converted into a comprehensive index, as has been done here, must be regarded as wide approximations. However in spite of the limitations it is of interest to make the comparison. The index arrived at by this method is:

1980 —	£1.00	1921 —	10.04
1975 —	1.96	1914 —	23.76
1970 —	3.61	1910 —	25.39
1963 —	4.90	1900 —	26.50
1960 —	5.33	1890 —	27.06
1950 —	7.42	1880 —	23.15
1946 —	8.99	1870 —	22.04
1938 —	15.22	1860 —	21.48
1930 —	15.04		

Confidence in this index is somewhat reduced by the common observation that for many commodities the 1980 pound is worth less than the 1930 shilling.

Allen Hugh
Apsley Mr.
Armstrong Mrs.
Auld Mussenden
Banks Mrs.
Bigger Miss
Blackwell Mrs.
Blow Dan
Broom Margaret
Brown John
Brown Wm.
Brown John
Brown Ann
Brown Mr.
Brown Wm.
Caldwell Mrs.
Campbell John
Cooper Jas.
Crawford A.
Donaldson Mrs.
Dorman John
Douglas Mrs.
Drennan Mrs.
Dunn Jas.
Dunbar John
Elder Mr.
Ewing Mr.
Faulkner Aban.
Finley Walter
Galon Mr.
Getty James
Gordon Mrs.
Grahams Jas.
Grahams Thos.
Gregg John
Gregg Wm.
Greg Thomas
Haliday Dr.
Hamilton Mrs.
Hamilton Miss

Hamilton Fr.
Hamilton Fr.
Hamilton Jno.
Hanna Robt.
Harper Robt.
Harvey Mrs.
Hathron Mrs.
Hay John
Hay Jno. Junr.
Henderson David
Herdman Robt.
Heyland Her.
Holmes Jn.
Hughes Jas.
Hunter Jno.
Irwin Thos.
Kennedy Jno.
Kinley Jas.
Kirkpatrick Alex.
Legg Mrs.
Linns Messrs.
Lyle Thos.
McBridge Margt.
McCabe Thos.
McCleary Robt.
McCormick Jno.
McIlwean Thos.
McKedy Mr.
McMaster Hugh
McTier Sml.
Magee Jas.
Manson D.
Martin Capt.
Mathers John
Mattear Dr.
Mattear Miss
Miller Is.
Mitchell Samuel
Montgomery C.
Montgomery Hugh

Neilson And.
Orr Mr.
Osborn Row.
Osborn Wm.
Panton Mrs. J.
Park Mrs.
Park David
Park James
Patterson Marthaw
Perrey Jas.
Rainey Jno.
Ramsey Wm.
Roberts C.
Robinson Jas.
Robinson John
Rice Marth.
Scott Mr.
Sharp Miss
Shaw Henry
Sinclair T.
Smith J.G.
Smith Robert
Smith Wid.
Smyth Robert
Stevenson Mr.
Stewart John
Stewart Wm.
Sykes Jno.
Taylor Jess
Wallace Jos.
Wallace Robt.
Ward Jno.
Ward Mark
Warnock Wm.
Wilson John
Wilson Wm.
Wilson Sml.

APPENDIX 9: LIST OF MEMBERS 1790 FROM DR. BRUCE'S MANUSCRIPT

Allen Miss, Mill Gate
Allen Mrs, Linenhall St.
Apsley Miss Elz, Castle St.
Bamber Geo, High St.
Bamber Miss, High St.
Beatty Stewart, Hercules Lane
Bigger Miss, Hercules Lane
Blackwell Mrs. W, Donegal St.
Brown Samuel, High St.
Brown W, Waring St.
Brown Jno, Linenhall St.
Brown Thos, Waring St.
Brown Jas.
Callwell Mrs, Bridge St.
Callwell John, Bridge St.
Callwell Robert, Bridge St.

Campbell John, Ann St.
Cochran, E.
Crombie Mrs, Donegal St.
Cumming John, Ann St.
Davidson Jas.
Donaldson Mrs, Bridge St.
Drennan Mrs, Donegal St.
Dunn Jas, Donegal St.
Dunn David, Donegal St.
Ewing J, Belfast Bank
Ferguson James, North St.
Ferguson James, Rosemary Lane
Clancy Jas.
Gordon Robt, Parade
Gordon D, Linenhall St.
Graham Mrs, Bridge St.

Graham Jno C, Bridge St.
Graham J.
Graham Thos.
Greg Thos, Gaw's Place
Greg Cun, Gaw's Place
Gregg Jno, Waring St.
Haliday Dr, Castle St.
Hamilton Miss J, Hercules Lane
Hamilton Jno, Belfast Bank
Haven Mrs, Hercules Lane
Hays Miss, Bridge St.
Henderson Capt. N, Hanover Quay
Herdman Robt, North St.
Hodgson Robt, Ann St.
Holmes Jno, Belfast Bank
Holmes Jas, Donegal St.
Houston Mrs, Linenhall St.
Houston Jno, Linenhall St.
Hunter Jno, Church Lane
Hyde Mrs, Parade
Hyndman Jas, High St.
Irwin W, Ann St.
Jackson Mrs, Waring St.
Joy Mrs, Linenhall`St.
Kairns Hugh, Parkmount
Kenby Mrs, High St.
Knox Geo.
Legg Miss, Bridge St.
Linn Robt, Skipper's Lane
Luke Jas, Donegal St.
Lyle Thos, High St.
McCleary Robt.
McCleary Robert, Bridge St.
McCormick Ed, Chichester Quay
McCreery Simon, North St.
McDowell Miss, High St.
McDonnell J, Bridge St.
McGregor A.
McKedy Mrs, High St.
McKibben Capt. J, Chichester Quay
McMaster P, High St.
McTier S, Cunningham's Row
Magee James, Bridge St.
Magee Wm, Bridge St.
Major Robt.
Manson David, Donegal St.
Mason Jas, New Brewry
Mathers Jno, Waring St.
Mattear Dr, High St.

Mattear Miss, Cunningham's Row
Mattear David, Castle St.
Maxwell Rainey, Grenville
Miller Isaac, Bridge St.
Milliken Thos, Donegal St.
Mills Mrs, Caddle's Entry
Mills Mrs, Rosemary Lane
Mitchell Samuel, Ann St.
Montgomery Hugh, Linenhall St.
Montgomery Robt, Arthur St.
Mulrea Wm, Church Lane
Murdock Jno, Bridge St.
Nichol Will, Pottinger's Entry
Oakman Jno.
Oakman W, Waring St.
Orr Alex, Linenhall St.
Osborne Rowland, Church Lane
Osborne R. Jun, Church Lane
Osborne W, Church Lane
Park Mrs, High St.
Park Mrs, High St.
Patterson Robt, Bridge St.
Patterson Jas.
Rabb Mrs, Rosemary Lane
Rainey Jno, Greenville
Rainey W, Greenville
Ramsey Wm, High St.
Roberts Chas, Waring St.
Robinson John
Robinson Mrs.
Scott Capt, High Street
Sharp Miss, High St.
Sinclair Miss, High St.
Sinclair Thos, Mill St.
Sinclair W, Mill St.
Smith Robt, Bridge St.
Smith Jno G, High St.
Steel Capt, Waring St.
Stevenson Robt, Donegal St.
Stevenson Jas, Chichester Quay
Thompson Arthur
Thompson Robt, Mile Water
Thompson Jno, Jennymount
Thompson Jno.
Watson David, Bridge St.
Ward Mark, High St.
Willis Mrs, Rosemary Lane
Wilson Robt, Parade
Wilson Wm, Donegal St.

APPENDIX 10: LIST OF MEMBERS WHO PAY STIPEND 1825

Ballantine Mrs.
Barklie Allen
Batt Mrs.
Black Henderson
Black Alex.
Black Mathew
Blackwell Mrs.
Boyd William
Boyd William
Burden William
Calwell Robert

Carruthers James
Chermside Thomas
Crawford Hugh
Creek Charles
Cumming Cllr.
Cunningham Mrs.
Cunningham J&T
Cunningham B.
Currell John
Davidson James
Delap Robert

Douglass James
Drennan Mrs.
Dunn Misses
Fergusin William
Ferguson Miss
Finlay William
Garrett Thomas
Gillies John
Graham Mrs.
Grainger James
Gregg John

Haliday Dr.
Hamilton Robt.
Hartley John
Haven Miss
Heron John
Hincks Rev. T.D.
Hodgson John
Holmes Mrs. R.
Holmes John
Houston John H.
Hylton Capt.
Hyndman Mrs. G.
Hyndman Mrs. A.
Joy George
Joy Henry
Kearns Mrs.
Lyle Mrs.
Lyle John
McAdam James
McAdam John
McCalmont Hugh
McCapin Wm.
McCleery John
McCluney Robert
McDonnell Alex.
McGee Mrs.
McIlveen G.
McKedy Miss

McTear David
McTier Mrs.
McTier Miss
Machan John
Magee William
Martin John
Miles Mrs.
Mitchell Alex.
Montgomery Jas.
Montgomery Miss
Montgomery Jas.
Montgomery Misses
Montgomery R.
Montgomery Mrs.
Montgomery Rev. H.
Moreland Alex.
Moreland Arthur
Mulrea William
Munster Paul
Napier William
Nicholson Mrs.
Orr William
Orr James
Patterson James
Patterson Misses
Patterson Robert
Radcliffe William
Read William

Riddel John
Rowan Mrs.
Russell William
Russel John
Seed Mrs.
Seed Wm.
Sinclair Mrs. W.
Sinclair Thomas
Sinclair John
Sloan George
Sloan John
Sloane William
Stavely James
Stevenson Mrs.
Stewart Mrs.
Stormont David
Smith Edward
Smith J.G.
Smith Miss
Telfair Robert
Telfair Misses
Tennent Wm.
Thomson Dr.
Ward John
White William
Whitla Francis
Wills Miss
Williamson Thos.

APPENDIX 11: LIST OF SEAT HOLDERS 1850

Allen W.J.C.
Adams John
Armstrong Mrs.
Barber Miss
Batt Miss
Black Alex
Blain Thomas
Bowles Chas.
Bowles Geo.
Boyd Robert
Boyd J.C.
Boyd Daniel
Bristow Jas.
Bristow Joseph
Brown Jas.
Bruce Mrs.
Bryson Wm.
Burden The Misses
Burden Dr. Wm.
Campbell Jn.
Carr James
Carruthers Jas.
Chermside Thos.
Coffey Jas.
Combe Jas.
Crozier Wm. J.
Cunningham Mrs.
Cunningham John
Currell John
Currell David

Dickson Ann Jane
Dickson Mrs.
Drennan Mrs.
Drennan Lenox
Drennan Dr. John
Dunbar Geo.
Dunn The Misses
Dunville John
Dunville William
Dunville Mrs. John Jn.
Ferguson Geo.
Garrett Henry
Garrett Mrs.
Grainger Miss
Grimshaw Edmund
Haffern Wm.
Hartley Wm.
Hartley Jn.
Henry Miss
Heron Rev. Wm.
Hincks Rev. Dr.
Hodgson Jn.
Home Wm.
Houston Mrs. B.
Hyndman Geo C.
Irwin Wm.
Johnson Henry
Johnson Mrs.
Johnson Thos B.
Kennedy John

Kennedy John
Kirker Wm.
Lowry Hugh
Luke Mrs.
McAdam Jas.
McAdam John
McAdam R.S.
McCance Mrs.
McCance David
McCaw J.F.
McDonnell Alex.
McGee Miss
McGee Miss M.A.
McKeady Misses
McKibben Dr. R.
McTear The Misses
McTear Geo.
Macrory Mrs.
Malcolm Dr. A.G.
Malcolm Mrs.
Malcolm W.H.
Marshall Dr. A.
Marshall Wm.
Martin John
May Mrs.
Miller Jane
Mitchell Alex.
Montgomery Alex.
Montgomery Miss
Montgomery Miss

Montgomery Robt.
Montgomery Miss
Moreland Miss
Munster Paul L.
Musgrave J.R.
Neill John R.
Oakman N.
Orr Alex.
Patterson Robt.
Porter Rev. J.S.
Reid Archibald
Rice Wm.

Riddel Wm.
Riddel Jn.
Ritchie Jas.
Robinson Mrs.
Rowan John
Russell John
Sherrard Conolly
Smith J.G.
Smith G.K.
Smith Mrs.
Smith Edward J.
Smyth Joseph

Stavely George
Stewart Miss
Sufferin Mrs.
Telfair Mrs.
Tennent Jas. T.
Thompson Miss Mary
Vance Mrs.
Ward Mrs.
Wilson Mrs.
Whitla Valentine
Whitla Francis

APPENDIX 12: LIST OF CONSTITUENTS 1875

Allen W.J.C.
Andrews Mrs.
Armstrong Mrs. C.D.
Arthur Miss M.
Baird Samuel
Baxter Richard
Baxter W.
Baxter R.
Bell Mrs.
Blackley Mrs.
Bowles Charles
Bowring Miss
Briggs Henry
Bruce James
Bruce Mrs.
Bruce Miss E.J.
Bruce Henry
Bryans John
Burden Dr. H.
Campbell John
Campbell Wm.
Campbell Miss
Campbell N.A.
Carley Mrs.
Carlisle John
Carr James
Carruthers Miss
Carruthers Miss J.
Cavan James
Charnock Mrs.
Cooper Mrs.
Creighton Mrs.
Cronne Jas.
Crooks Geo.
Crozier W.J.
Darbishire H.
Darbishire J.M.
Davison John
Dempster James
Dickson R.
Dickson Mrs.
Dickson James
Dixon Mrs.
Dobbin Wm.
Dobbin A.C.
Drennan Lennox
Drennan Dr. John
Drummond Mrs.

Dugan J.J.
Dunn Miss
Dunn John
Ferguson Miss
Finlay John
Firth George
Fleming Henry
Forsythe Mrs.
Gamble Mrs.
Gault John
Gawn James
Gillespie John
Goldstein Mrs.
Gordon Dr. Alex.
Graham W.
Graham Thomas
Graham James
Gray Mrs. R.
Gray James A.
Greer Mrs.
Greer W.H.
Haffern William
Hall Samuel
Hamilton W.T.
Harland E.J.
Hill Rev. George
Hinchey William
Home Wm.
Johnston T.B.
Johnston Alexander
Kennedy John
Kirker Archibald
Kirkpatrick Mrs.
Laird Marshall
Lawson John
Ledlie Mrs. G.
Leslie James
L'Estrange Thomas
Little Fredrick
Lowe Miss
Lowry Mrs.
Lyle Hugh
MacAdam R.S.
McAneaney Miss
McCance Miss
McCance Miss M.
McCance Miss J.
McCaul Joseph

McCaw Alex
McCaw James F.
McClelland Thomas
McClelland Miss
McClenaghan James
McCloy Joseph
McCracken R.
McCrum Robert
McCullough Thomas
McErvill Edward
McErvill Thomas
McErvill James
McFadden Mrs.
McFadden James
McGee Miss
McKeag Miss
McKeen John
McKinstry Miss
McLaughlin Miss
McMullen Elizabeth
McNinch Robert
McNinch William
McNinch James Watt
McQuitty Thomas
McRoberts Henry
McTear David
McTear George
McTear J.S.
McTear Miss
McTear Miss F.M.
McTear Miss
McTear Miss A.C.
Mairs Thomas
Major James
Malcolm Mrs. A.G.
Malcolm W.H.
Malcolm Mrs.
Martin John
Martin David
May Mrs.
Moore James
Mulligan Mrs.
Murray Henry
Murray Robert
Musgrave J.R.
Neeson Mrs.
Neill James
Nelson John

Oakman Nicholas
Palmer Benjamin
Palmer W.J.
Palmer James
Parkhill H.
Patterson W.H.
Patterson R.L.
Patterson D.C.
Patterson Mrs.
Pile Francis
Porter Rev. J.S.
Porter A.M. QC.
Quee Patrick
Rankin Mrs.
Rice Mrs. Jane
Riddel Hill
Riddel Samuel
Riddel William
Riddel Miss
Riddel Miss I.
Riddel Miss E.
Ritchie Thomas
Robb Alexander

Roberts Walter
Robertson William
Roche Mrs.
Roddy Hugh
Rogers John
Rogers Thomas
Runge John H.
Russell J.W.
Scott Miss
Sherrard The Misses
Sinclair Johnston
Sinclair George
Smith Mrs.
Smith Miss
Smith George K.
Smith J. Gault
Smith Mrs. H.C.
Smyth Dr. Brice
Smyth Miss
Smyth Miss A.J.
Spackman William
Steen Henry
Steenson James

Stewart Miss
Stewart Thomas
Taylor A. O'D.
Templeton Robert
Templeton Andrew
Templeton Robert
Thomas H.F.
Thompson Miss
Thompson Robert
Thompson Thomas
Todd Miss M.C.
Ward John
Ward F.D.
Ward Mrs.
Whitla Miss
Whitla Mrs.
Williamson David
Williamson Joseph
Williamson James
Woodside Samuel

APPENDIX 13: ROLL OF CONSTITUENTS 1900

Alexander Mrs, Cedar Ave.
Andrews Mrs, Ardoyne House
Andrews George, Ardoyne House
Armstrong C, 4 Chilworth Buildings
Armstrong Mrs. Farncham, Marlborough Park
Armstrong Miss, Farncharm, Marlborough Park
Armstrong Miss J. Farncham, Marlborough Park
Baxter Richard, Chlorine
Baxter William, Chlorine
Benn Miss, Derryvolgie Avenue
Bennett William, Cremorne, Strandtown
Birkmyre McA. A.
Blyth Wm, 38 Parkmount St.
Boas Ernest, Bangor
Boyd W.S, Ravenscroft, Bloomfield
Bruce Jas, Thorndale
Bruce Miss, The Farm
Bruce Miss C, The Farm
Bruce Miss E, The Farm
Bruce Miss J.E. The Farm
Bulmer David, 4 Rosetta Gardens
Bulmer Mrs, 4 Rosetta Gardens
Burnett J.R. 46 Elmwood Ave.
Campbell Miss, Windsor Ave.
Campbell Miss M, Windsor Ave.
Carlisle Mrs, Ashburn, Sydenham
Carr Jas, Windsor Ave.
Carr A.H.R. Windsor Ave.
Carr John, Windsor Ave.
Carr S.C.N. Windsor Ave.
Carr Miss A.M. Windsor Ave.
Carruthers Miss, 9 Claremont St.

Carruthers Miss J, 9 Claremont St.
Charnock Mrs, 6 Lower Crescent
Chermside Miss, Albion Place
Clarke Mrs, 2 Connaught Tce.
Cleland Alex, 34 Orient Gardens
Cronne James, 6 Duferin Tce. Burmah St.
Crymble J, 224 York St.
Cunningham Dr C.M. Rostellan, Malone Road
Cunningham Miss, Malone Road
Curran Mrs, 2 Linden Gardens, Cliftonville
Darbishire Herbert, St. Margret's Windsor Park
Darbishire Mrs, St. Margret's Windsor Park
Darbishire Miss M, St. Margret's Windsor Park
Davidson James, Windsor Park
Dickson Miss, 91 Wilmont Tce.
Dickson Robert, 91 Wilmont Tce.
Dickson John, Lauriston Knock
Dunn Miss, 18 College Green
Erskine Joseph R, 4 Eia Street
Ferguson Henry, 5 Nut Grove, North Parade
Ferguson Miss, 16 Clifton St.
Forsythe Miss, 35 Castlereagh Place
Frame John, Knock
Gamble Mrs, 64 Apsley Place
Gault Mrs, 85 York St.
Gault Robert, 50 Elmwood Ave.
Gibson Jas. M, 77a Divis Street
Gilmore Hugh, 13 Sheridan St.
Glasie Mrs, Bristol St.

Gordon Rev. A, Memorial Hall, Manchester
Gordon Christopher, 10 Elmwood Ave.
Gracey Miss M.A., 5 Marlborough Park Tce.
Graham Jas, University Tce.
Gray Robert, 22 Balfour Ave.
Hall Alex, 23 Paxton St. Templemore Ave.
Hall Wm, Upton Tce. Hannahstown Rd.
Hamilton Mrs, Lennoxvale
Hamilton W.T., Lennoxvale
Hampton Isaac, Eagle Hall, Hampton Park
Hayes Miss, 297 Fern Tce. Hillman St.
Hill A.C., Landguard House, Cliftonville Ave.
Hill Mrs, Landguard House, Cliftonville Ave.
Hill Geo, Spring Vale House, Springfield
Hodges J.F.W., Galwally Park
Hunter H.B., 22 Cliftonpark Ave.
Hunter Jn, Victoria Gardens, Windsor Park
Hyndman Dr. H., Windsor Ave.
Johnston Jn, 15 Richmond Crescent
Johnston Wm, 6 Rosemount Gds.
Kell Wm, Ulidia, Skegoniel Ave.
Kennedy Wm, Belvidere, Church Rd, Knock
Kilpatrick A., 28 Coburg St. Willowfield
Kirker Arch. M., Craigavad
Kirker Miss, Norbrae, Kirkliston Drive
Knox Mrs, 27 Jaffa St.
Laird Mrs, 56 Crumlin Road
L'Estrange Thos, 7 Howard St.
Lindsay Miss, Victoria Gds. Windsor Park
Little Mrs, Greenisland
Lowry J.F., 108 Eglantine Ave.
Lowry Chas. R., 35 Castlereagh Place
Luke Miss, 23 Kinbella Ave.
Luke Fred, 23 Kinbella Ave.
Luke Wm, 23 Kinbella Ave.
McAdam A.B., Glengormley House, Whitewell
McAnally C, 30 Morelands Row, Castlereagh Rd.
McBride Thos, 20 Atlantic Ave.
McCafferty Wm, 86 Mountcollyer Ave.
McCalmont Mrs J.T., 257 Sundridge Terrace, M'pottinger
McCammon Mrs, 14 Glendore St.
McCann Alex, The Limes, Annadale Park
McCaw Geo. C, 40 Elmwood Ave.
McCaw Mrs, 40 Elmwood Ave.
McCaw Leo C.D., 31 Wellesley Ave.
McCaw Miss, 31 Wellesley Ave.
McCaw Miss L., 31 Wellesley Ave.
McClenaghan Miss, 27 Roseleigh St., Cliftonpark Ave.
McCloy Jos, 6 Kenbella Ave.
McCrum Robt, 18 India St.
McCrum Robt, 31a Wellington Place
McCrum Sml, 73 Wellesley Ave.
McClure H.O., 18 William St. South

McDowell Miss, 45 Hopefield Ave.
McDonnell Mrs, 22 Eia St.
McErvel Jas, Glenburn, Holywood
McErvel Thos, 2 Victoria Tce, Bangor
McFadden W.H., 4 Castleton Tce.
McFadden Mrs, 4 Castleton Tce.
McFerran Mrs, 21 Brookill Ave.
McGiffen Robt, 6 Duncairn Terrace
McKeag Miss, Knockbracken
McKisack Jas, 12 Mountcharies
McKisack Miss, 12 Mountcharles
McKisack Mrs, 12 Mountcharles
McLean Jas. N, 25 Courtney Tce. Lisburn Rd.
McMaster Jn, 16 Delhi St.
McMullan Isaac, St. Mary's Tce.
McMurray Ed, Marlborough Park
McMurray Geo, Myrtle Cottage, Bangor
McMurray Mrs. G, Myrtle Cottage, Bangor
McMurray Mrs, 6 St. John's Park, Ballynafeigh
McMurray Thos. H, Dunluce, Rosetta Pk.
McNinch Wm, 39 Lonsdale St.
McQuoid Jas, The Mount, Mountpottinger
McTear J.S., Groom Villas, Bangor
McTear Miss, The Cedars, Knock
McTear Miss F.M., The Cedars, Knock
McTear Miss E, Ard Greenan, Cavehill Rd.
McWilliams Jas, 4 Castlereagh Place
Magill Jas, 137 Old Lodge Road
Malcolm Bowman, Inver Ashley Park, Antrim Rd.
Malcolm Mrs, 21 Hughenden Tce.
Malcolm Miss, 21 Hughenden Tce.
Malcolm Mrs. A.G., 5 Hughenden Tce.
Manderson A.H., 3 Ashley Ave., Lisburn Rd.
Marshall Miss J, 27 Duncairn Gardens
Martin Lowrie, 17 Fitzwilliam Ave.
Mercer Miss, 24 Windsor Rd.
Mateer Jn, 6 Shamrock St.
Matthews Mrs, 46 Dock St.
May Thos, Willowfield St.
Milligan Jn, 72 Albert St.
Moore Jas, 17 Donegall Place
Moore Dr. Jas, 11 College Sq. North
Moore Mrs, 3 Thorn Tce, Bloomfield Ave.
Mulligan Miss, Sydenham Park, Strandtown
Murray Robt, Ashby, Malone Rd.
Murray Miss, 5 Marlborough Park Tce.
Napier Miss, 10 Elmwood Ave.
Neill Jas, 10 Wilmont Tce.
Neill Sharman D, Marlborough Park
Nelson John, 5 Strangmore Tce, Crumlin Rd.
Nelson Jas. G, St. Etienne Tce., Lisburn Rd.
Nelson Miss, Marlborough Park
Nixon Mrs, 3 Chilworth Buildings
Orr Jas. P, Malone Park
Orr Miss, Ballylesson, Lisburn
Patterson, E.F., Adelaide Park

Patterson Mrs. E.F., Adelaide Park
Patterson Mrs. R, Malone Park
Patterson Robt, Malone Park
Pink Sml, 42 Agnes St.
Porter Drummond, Marlborough Park
Porter Miss, 16 College Sq. East
Rea Miss Lindores, Ormeau Road
Rea Jas, 24 Outram St.
Reid Miss, 23 Paxton St. Templemore Ave.
Rice Mercer, The Loop, Castlereagh Rd.
Riddell Miss, Beechmount
Riddell Miss I, Beechmount
Riddell Mrs, Ard Greenan, Cavehill Rd.
Riddel Sml, Beechmount
Ritchie Thos, Royal Terrace
Robb Miss A, 236 Newtownards Road
Robb Mrs, 236 Newtownards Road
Robertson Wm, Netherleigh, Strandtown
Roche Ed. B, 1 Fortwilliam Terrace
Roche H.G., 1 Fortwilliam Terrace
Roche Mrs, 1 Fortwilliam Terrace
Roddy Hugh, 3 Thorn Tce. Bloomfield Ave.
Rogers Fred. H, Windsor Ave.
Rogers Jn, Windsor Ave.
Rowan Miss, Botanic Ave.
Russell Mrs, 4 Dunedin Terrace
Scott Miss, 31a Wellington Place
Scott Miss S, 31a Wellington Place
Service Miss E, 21 Landscape Terrace
Service Wm, 28 Avonbeg St.

Simonton Jn, 122 Clifton Park Ave.
Sinclair Geo, 114 Wellwood Place
Smith Jn, Ballinasloe
Smyth Dr. Brice, University Square
Spackman Mrs, 25 Eglantine Ave.
Stevenson Geo, Fairburn, Knock
Stevenson Miss, Fairburn, Knock
Stevenson Miss S, Fairburn, Knock
Stewart Misses, 11 India St.
Stewart Miss C, 32 Canning St.
Stewart Miss Jane, 32 Canning St.
Stewart Miss J, 32 Canning St.
Stewart Thos, 15 Suir St, Oldpark Rd.
Thomas T.C., 53 Botanic Ave.
Todd Miss M.C., 297 Fern Tce. Hillman St.
Townsley Wm, 8 Upper Newtownards Rd.
Traill Mrs, 2 Lissa Villa, Whitehead
Traill Miss, 2 Lissa Villa, Whitehead
Wallace Jn, 48 St. Ives Gardens
Walmsley Rev. D. Redburn, Adelaide Park
Ward Francis D, Malone Park
Ward Geo G, Redlands, Adelaide Park
Ward Jn, Lennoxvale
Wharton Wm, 15 Donegall Ave.
Williamson Jas, 118 Nelson St.
Williamson Miss, 22 Eia St.
Wilson Mrs, 4 Hopefield Terrace
Wood W.H., 13 Arthur Tce., Antrim Road
Wright Robert, 7 Eccles St.

APPENDIX 14: ROLL OF CONSTITUENTS 1925

Alexander Miss J, 5 Glenwith Drive
Alexander Miss A, 5 Glenwith Drive
Allen Mrs S, 59 Farnham St.
Allison S.H., Cliftonville Rod.
Allison Mrs, Cliftonville Rd.
Arbuckle Joseph, 16 Danube St.
Arbuckle Miss, 16 Danube St.
Armstrong C.D., Rosebank, Windsor Ave.
Armstrong Miss, Marlborough Park
Armstrong Miss J, Marlborough Park
Barnes R.A., 13 Ravenhill Park Gardens
Barnes Mrs. R.S., 13 Ravenhill Park
   Gardens
Barry Mrs, 282 Ormeau Road
Bell J.J. Dunkell, Castle Ave.
Blair Mrs, 54 Copperfield St.
Blair J.G., 3 Victoria Gdns.
Blair Mrs. J.G., 3 Victoria Gdns.
Blyth Mrs, 4 Roosevelt St.
Blyth Miss C, 4 Roosevelt St.
Blyth Miss L, 4 Roosevelt St.
Blyth Campbell, 66 Donegall Road
Boas Mrs, 7 College Gdns.
Boas Miss, 7 College Gdns.
Boyd W.A., Artana, Dromara
Boyd Mrs, 38 Castleton Gdns.
Bredford Miss M, 194 Duncairn Gdns.
Brierley Mrs, Cliftonville Rd.
Brown James, 138 Woodvale Road

Brown Mrs. J, 138 Woodvale Road
Brown Mrs. T, 7 Dock St.
Bruce Miss J.E., The Farm
Burnett Mrs, 32 Eglantine Ave.
Campbell Mrs. R, 22 College Gdns.
Cardwell Mrs. Alton, Helen's Bay
Carlisle Wm, 87 Castlereagh St.
Carlisle Miss, 87 Castlereagh St.
Carlisle Miss, 24 Belgrave Sq., London
Carr A.H.R., Deramore Park
Carr Thos. J, Deramore Drive
Carr John, 10 Lennoxvale
Carr S.C.N., Windsor Ave.
Carr Miss A.M., Windsor Ave.
Carr Miss E, Windsor Ave.
Clarke F.E., 34 University Ave.
Clarke Miss O, 34 University Ave.
Clarke R, 9 Pacific Ave.
Craig Mrs, 30 Eia Street
Crawford Miss E, 28 Newington St.
Creighton Mrs, 10 Glendower St.
Cronne Miss J, 8 Delhi St.
Crozier Miss C.
Cunningham Miss, 11 Malone Ave.
Davidson Miss F, Bryansford
Davidson Mrs. James, Wandsworth Rd.
Donnan Miss J, 27 Tavanagh St.
Eakins Chas R, 6 Whitewell Crescent
Eakins Mrs, 6 Whitewell Crescent

Ellis Mrs, Verdun, Crumlin Rd.
Ellis Moses, Brookland Villas, Lisburn Rd.
Ellis Mrs. M, Brookland Villas, Lisburn Rd.
Elston Mrs, Waterloo Gardens
Erskine J.R., 38 Castleton Gdns.
Ervine David, 16 Grampian Ave.
Ervine Mrs, Knock Rd.
Ervine Miss M, Knock Rd.
Ervine Sam, Knock Rd.
Ervine Mrs. S, Knock Rd.
Ferguson Mrs, Cyprus Park
Forsythe Miss L, 60 Ardenlee Ave.
Fox John, Bloomfield Gdns.
Galloway A, 13 Botanic Ave.
Garrett Miss M, 11 Malone Ave.
Gibson Mrs, 26 Salisbury Ave.
Gilliland J.H., 33 Gresham St.
Gledhill Mrs, Cliftonville Rd.
Gordon Eustance, 105 Main St. Bangor
Gordon Christopher, 105 Main St. Bangor
Gourley Miss, Whitewell
Gracey Miss, 47 Botanic Avenue
Graham Miss, Ormiston Gdns.
Graham D, 21 Willowholme St.
Graham Mrs, 21 Willowholme St.
Hall A.E., Crumlin Rd.
Hall Mrs, 25 Glantane St.
Hall Miss C, 25 Glantane St.
Hall Miss G, 25 Glantane St.
Hall Mrs, 10 Stranmillis Road
Hall Wm, Crumlin Rd.
Hamilton W.T., Lennoxvale
Hanley W.G., 165 Alexandra Park Ave.
Hanley Mrs. A, 165 Alexandra Park Ave.
Hanley Miss, 165 Alexandra Park Ave.
Hayhurst Mrs, Cadogan Park
Hewitt Wm, 71 High St.
Hewitt Miss M, 71 High St.
Hewitt R, 67 The Mount
Hill Wm, 20 Edlingham St.
Hill Albert C, Ballyholme
Hill Mrs, Ballyholme
Hill Mrs, 41 Martinez Ave.
Hill Thomas, 45 Ardenlee Drive
Hill Geo Y, Chichester Park
Hill Mrs. G.Y., Chichester Park
Hill Miss G.M., Chichester Park
Hill Miss E.J., Chichester Park
Hill Miss E.C., Chichester Park
Hill Norman, Chichester Park
Hume Miss, 108 Mrytlefield Park
Humphrey Jas, 43 Jaffa St.
Hunter Wm, 24 Trevelyan Terrace
Hunter Mrs. W, 24 Trevelyan Terrace
Hunter Albert, 123 Cliftonpark Ave.
Hutchinson Mrs, 122 Woodvale Road
Hutton Robert, 153 Ulsterville Ave.
Hutton Miss, The Farm
Hutton Joseph, 16 Agincourt St.
Jardine Miss, 15 Cliftonville Ave.
Jennings Victor G, Sandown Road
Johnston R.H., 21 Wandsworth Road
Johnstone Mrs, 6 Victoria Gardens

Keenan Miss, 45 Cooke St.
Keiller W, 7 Abercorn Terrace
Kelly Mrs, 36 Grace Ave.
Kelly Miss I, 36 Grace Ave.
Kennedy R, 7 Victoria Terrace
Kennedy Alan, Ingram, Lisburn
Kennedy Miss, Hawthornden Road
Kennedy Robert, 29 Sandhurst Gdns.
Kennedy Robert, 29 Sandhurst Gdns.
Kennedy Miss D, 29 Sandhurst Gdns.
Kennedy Miss E, 29 Sandhurst Gdns.
Kilpatrick W, 67 Portallo St.
Kirker Mrs.
Laird Wm, 16 Woodland Ave.
Laird, R.M. Gratan, Hampton Park
Laird Miss D. Gratan, Hampton Park
Laird Jas. A, 16 Glandore Ave.
Laird Miss M, 16 Glandore Ave.
Logan Miss, 5 Mountcollyer Ave.
Lowry J. Fraser, 45 Eglantine Ave.
Lowry Mrs, 45 Eglantine Ave.
Lowry Miss, 45 Eglantine Ave.
Lowry S.G.N., College Park Ave.
Lowry Mrs, College Park Ave.
Luke Miss, 12 Salisbury Ave.
Luke Wm, 12 Salisbury Ave.
Lusk Jas, Fairview Carnmoney
Lusk Martha, Fairview, Carnmoney
Lusk Robert P, Fairview, Carnmoney
Lusk Thomas G, Fairview, Carnmoney
Lusk Wm. J, Fairview, Carnmoney
Lusk Fred, Fairview, Carnmoney
Lusk Herbert, Fairview, Carnmoney
McAlonen James, 116 Cliftonpark Ave.
McBride H, 32 Welland St.
McBride Thos, 20 Atlantic Ave.
McCafferty Wm, 15 Glanleam Drive
McCafferty Mrs. Wm, 15 Glenleam Drive
McCafferty Jas R, 40 Southport St.
McCafferty Joseph, 7 Parkside Gdns.
McCafferty W.H., 15 Glenleam Drive
McCalmont Miss, 257 Sunridge Tce.
McCalmont Miss M, 257 Sunridge Tce.
McCandless Mrs, 45 Victoria St.
McCann Alexander, 21 Church Lane
McCann Mrs, 21 Church Lane
McCaw Miss, 31 Wellesley Ave.
McCaw Miss L, 31 Wellesley Ave.
Maclenaghan James, 49 Avoca St.
McCloy Miss, 14 Norfolk Drive
McCloy Miss, 6 Salisbury Ave.
McClughan J.W., 4 Wellington Cres.
McCrum Robert, 118 Marlborough Park
Central
McCrum Ivan, 118 Marlborough Park
Central
McCrum Wm, 118 Marlborough Park
Central
McCrum Miss D, 118 Marlborough Park
Central
McDonnell Miss, 37 The Mount
McDowell Miss, 45 Hopefield Ave.
McFadden Mrs, 8 Adelaide Park

149

McGrogan Mrs, 32 Canning St.
McKee Wm, 441 Springfield Road
McKelvey John, 9 Isadore Ave.
Mackenzie John, 40 Marlborough Park
McKeown A.B., 39 Adelaide Ave.
McKeown Mrs, 39 Adelaide Ave.
McKisack Miss, 38 Botanic Ave.
McKisack James, 9 Mountpleasant
McKisack Chas J, 9 Mountpleasant
McKisack A.M., 9 Mountpleasant
McMurray Thomas H, 26 Cliftonville Ave.
McMurray Charles, 39 Farnham St.
McMurray Charles Jun, 39 Farnham St.
McMurray Mrs. George, 12 Eglantine St.
McNeill Henry, 28 Summer St.
McNeill Archd, 54 Belmont Ave.
McNinch R.A., 12 Rathgar Street
McNinch H.A., 12 Rathgar Street
McNinch R.J., 12 Rathgar Street
McRobert Wm, 61 Wellington Park
McRobert Mrs, 61 Wellington Park
McRoberts Mrs, 16 Victoria Gardens
McTear Mrs. F.M., Creevelea, Knock
Magill G, 11 Victoria Gardens
Major Mrs. Ulai, Holywood
Malcolm Bowman, Inver Ashley Park
Malcolm Mrs. B., Inver Ashley Park
Malcolm Miss, 21 Hughenden Ave.
Malcolm Miss F, 21 Hughenden Ave.
Martin Robert, Ravenhill Park
Martin Miss E.P., Ravenhill Park
Martin William, 11 Colenso Parade
Martin James, 32 Pine St.
Matthews Mrs, 33 Crosscollyer St.
Mayes Mrs. T.H., 101 Malone Ave.
Mercer Miss M.E., 16 Meadowbank St.
Milliken J, 153 Divis St.
Montgomery Joseph, 1 Maryville Park
Montgomery Henry, 1 Maryville Park
Montgomery Miss N, 1 Maryville Park
Montgomery Miss K, 1 Maryville Park
Montgomery Tom, 1 Maryville Park
Moore Dr. Jas, University Road
Moore Mrs, University Road
Moore Ken M, 17 Donegall Place
Moore A.R., Edlingham St.
Morrison J.S., 3 Abingdon St.
Morrison Mrs, 3 Abingdon St.
Morrow W.F.B., 7 Cliftonpark Ave.
Morrow W.A.J., Clifton Street
Morrow H.P., 4 Irwin Ave.
Morton Mrs. Jas, 43 Jaffa St.
Mulligan Miss C, 9 Kerr St., Portrush
Nelson John, 10 Damascus St.
Newman Wm, 34 Fitzroy Ave.
Newman Miss Nan, 34 Fitzroy Ave.
Newman Tom, 34 Fitzroy Ave.
Newman H.F., Station House, Bloomfield
Orr H.J.F., King's Road
Orr Mrs, King's Road
Orr P.B., 51 Osborne Gdns.
Orr Mrs., Malone Park
Parker Thos, 121 Roden St.

Park Miss E, 121 Roden St.
Parker Miss L, 121 Roden St.
Parker Miss M, 121 Roden St.
Parker Miss A, 121 Roden St.
Patterson C.D., 25 Rugby Rd.
Patterson Miss H, 25 Rugby Rd.
Patterson Mrs, 16 Danube St.
Pedlow W.J., 35 Oldpark Ave.
Pirrie Vicountess, 24 Belgrave Sq. London
Pirrie Miss L, 28 Newington St.
Porter Miss, 3 Eileen Gdns.
Pringle Geo, 172 Albertbridge Road
Purcell Mrs R.D., Finaghy Park
Rea Mrs, 33 Roseleigh St.
Rea F.W., 24 Rosevale St.
Rea Mrs, 24 Rosevale St.
Riddel Mrs, Glastonbury Ave.
Ritchie Miss, 82 Marlborough Park North
Ritchie Miss E.L., 82 Marlborough Park
North
Ritchie Miss M.G., 82 Marlborough Park
North
Ritchie Miss A.L., Marlborough Park
North
Robinson Wm, 53 Lavinia St.
Roche Edmund B, 75 Eglantine Ave.
Roche Henry G, Sans Souci Park
Roche Miss, Sans Souci Park
Rogers Miss, 22 Derryvolgie Park
Rossington Rev. H.J., Cadogan Park
Rossington Mrs, Cadogan Park
Rowan Miss, 124 Great Victoria St.
Russell Mrs, 1 Buckingham St.
Russell Miss L, 1 Buckingham St.
Russell Mrs, Whitehouse
Russell Alfred, 64 Ravenhill Park
Russell Alfred Jun, 64 Ravenhill Park
Russell Miss E, 64 Ravenhill Park
Salthouse E, 172 Albertbridge Road
Scott Miss, 4 University Terrace
Scott Miss H, 4 University Terrace
Scott Robert, 60 Ardenlee Ave.
Scott James, 33 Manor St.
Scott Wm, 33 Manor St.
Service Miss, 29 Cardigan Drive
Service Mrs, 36 Lecumpher St.
Shaw Miss J, Lisburn Rd.
Simonton Mrs, Sheelah Malone Pk.
Simonton Miss, Sheelah Malone Pk.
Simonton Montague, 34 Tate's Ave.
Smith Miss, 16 Dunluce Ave.
Smyth Dr. Malcolm B, 20 University Sq.
Spence Jas, 112 Donnybrook St.
Stewart John, 209 Hillman St.
Stewart Thomas, 8 Derg St.
Stewart Robert, 96 Hillview St.
Stewart Mrs, 34 Pacific Ave.
Stewart Miss L, 34 Pacific Ave.
Stevenson Miss, Kensington Rd.
Tate W.J., 27 Hogarth St.
Tate Joseph, 14 Annalee St.
Taylor Mrs, 109 Duncairn Gdns.
Thomas Trevor C, Helens Bay

Thompson John, 52 Duncairn Gdns.
Traill Miss, 2 Lissa Villa, Whitehead
Wallace Mrs. C, Chichester Park
Wallace Mrs, 63 Dublin Road
Ward Mrs. G.G., Craigavad
Wilkinson John, North Road
Wilkinson R, 12 India St.
Wilson Wm, 29 Ballarat St.

Wilson Miss A, 29 Ballarat St.
Wilson Mrs. M.J., 93 Upper Meadow St.
Wilson Mrs, 48 Fernwood St.
Wood W.H., Donegall Park Avenue
Worth Ernest, 2 Shandon Park W. Bangor
Wright Robert, 7 Eccles St.
Wright Miss F., 7 Eccles St.
Wright T.H., 7 Eccles St.

APPENDIX 15: ROLL OF CONSTITUENTS 1950

Allison S.H., Rock Cottage, Orlock
Allison Mrs, Rock Cottage, Orlock
Arbuckle Joseph, 556 Crumlin Road
Arbuckle Norman J.T., 28 Southwell Rd.,
   Bangor
Armstrong Miss, Farnham, Marlborough
   Park South
Barnes R.A. Grafton, Kensington Rd.
Barnes Mrs. Grafton, Kensington Rd.
Barry W.W., 31 Cranmore Ave.
Beattie W.R., 32 Kensington Rd.
Beattie Mrs, 32 Kensington Rd.
Bell J. Johnston, 69 Lansdowne Rd.
Bell W.R., 85 Sunnyhill Park Dunmurry
Blair John G, 9 Ben Madigan Park S.
Blair Mrs. J.G., 9 Ben Madigan Park S.
Blythe A.F., 1 Slievecool Park
Blythe Mrs, 1 Slievecool Park
Blythe Brian, 1 Slievecool Park
Boas Mrs. M, 31 Sans Souci Park
Boas Miss M, 31 Sans Souci Park
Boyd H, 77 Portallo St.
Boyd S. Wilson, Tara Marino
Boyd Mrs. S.W., Tara Marino
Brown James, Silverstream, Comber Rd.,
   Dundonald
Brown Mrs. J, 2 Ulverston St.
Browne J. Nelson, 2 Spring Gardens
Campbell N, 35 Moorfield St.
Campbell J.A., 76 Rugby Rd.
Campbell Mrs. J, 4 Bandon St.
Carr T.J. Blythswood, Deramore Drive
Carr John, 10 Lennoxvale
Carr S.C.N., Rathowen, Windsor Ave.
Carruth Miss E, 650 Springfield Rd.
Carruth Miss E, 650 Springfield Rd.
Castellano G, 60 Ladas Drive
Castellano Mrs. G, 60 Ladas Drive
Castellano N. Rosemary, Priory Park,
   Finaghy
Castellano Mrs. N. Rosemary, Priory
   Park, Finaghy
Chambers Mrs. M.E., 22 Cabin Hill
   Gardens
Chambers Miss E.V., 22 Cabin Hill
   Gardens
Chambers J.A., 19 Cranmore Park
Clarke, Mrs. R, 6 Grasmere Gardens
Clarke Miss H, 6 Grasmere Gardens
Clyde J, 38 Silverstream Gardens
Clyde Mrs. J, 38 Silverstream Gardens

Cobain Miss, 497 Antrim Road
Colvin Mrs. V, 687 Lisburn Road
Cotter Miss M, 20 Brookvale Ave.
Coughlan G.T., 161 Cavehill Rd.
Coughlan Mrs, 161 Cavehill Rd.
Creighton Miss M, 10 Glendower St.
Creighton Wm, 50 Thames St.
Davidson Miss F.J., The Nest, Bryansford
Doonan Wm, 59 Kimberley St.
Doonan Jas, 59 Kimberley St.
Doonan Miss M, 59 Kimberley St.
Doonan Miss L, 59 Kimberley St.
Duff Mrs, 9 Silverstream Gdns.
Duff Miss M, 9 Silverstream Gdns.
Duffin The Misses, Summerhill,
   Stranmillis
Dunn Miss M, 16 Ravenhill Park
Elmes John, 13 Mount Vernon Pk.
Elmes Mrs, 13 Mount Vernon Pk.
Elston Mrs. H.G., Maitlands, Waterloo
   Gardens
Erskine The Misses, Clifton Lodge,
   Cliftonville Road
Ervine Mrs. R, Altafort, Downshire Rd.
Ervine Mrs. D, 52 Cabin Hill Park
Ervine S, 245 Upper Newtownards Road
Ervine Mrs. S, 245 Upper Newtownards
   Road
Ervine S, 3 Knock Road
Ervine Mrs. S, 3 Knock Road
Ervine Miss M, 11 Knock Road
Evans W, 89 Highfield Drive
Ferguson W.J., 28 Brussels St.
Fieldhouse Mrs. W, 1 Ardgreenan Mt.
Fisher Mrs. E, Shanacloon, Upper
   Malone
Foote Joseph, 55 Oakland Ave.
Foote Mrs. J, 55 Oakland Ave.
Forsythe Miss L, Marathon, Cushendall
Foulds Mrs. F, 43 Malone Road
Frame Miss K, 19 Castlereagh St.
Frame Mrs. M, 66 Martinez Ave.
Gibson Miss J, 26 Salisbury Ave.
Gibson John, 14 Drew St.
Gibson Mrs. J, 14 Drew St.
Gordon Eustace, 105 Main St., Bangor
Goslin Mrs. R.W., 47 Martinez Ave.
Graham Miss M, 5 Cabin Hill Park
Graham D, 67 Onslow Parade
Graham Mrs, 67 Onslow Parade
Graham Mrs. J, 69 Ulsterville Ave.

Green Miss C, 51 Beresford St.
Hall Mill C, 12 Dunowen Gdns.
Hall Mrs. M.I., 12 Dunowen Gdns.
Hall A.E., Stoneyridge, Quarry Road
Hall Mrs. A.E., Stoneyridge, Quarry Road
Hall Miss I, Stoneyridge, Quarry Road
Hall Miss A, Stoneyridge, Quarry Road
Hall Miss M, 4 Kenbella Pde.
Hamill E, 11 Knock Road
Hamill Mrs. E, 11 Knock Road
Hamilton Miss, 15a Eastleigh Drive
Hamilton Wm, 1 Artana St.
Hamilton Mrs, 1 Artana St.
Hanna Miss J, 44 Oldpark Ave.
Harvey Mrs. J.B., Elgin Rd., Calcutta
Heeson Mrs. J.W., 16 Remer St., Crewe
Hermin Mrs. A, 147 Alliance Ave.
Hester Mrs. E.V.C., 7 Lawrence St.
Hewitt Miss R, 67 The Mount
Hill Mrs. H, Kings Road, Knock
Hill Mrs. H.R., 81 Salisbury Ave.
Hillis Miss, 55 Oakland Ave.
Hillis Miss A, 55 Oakland Ave.
Hobart H, 6 Slievedarragh Park
Humphrey J, 12 Woodvale Parade
Humphrey Mrs. J, 69 Ulsterville Gardens
Hunter A, 93 Priory Park
Hutton Mrs, 9 Agincourt Ave.
Hutton Miss A.E., 9 Agincourt Ave.
Hutton Robert, Portland Avenue,
   Glengormley
Irvine Mrs. J.M., 9 Mountpleasant
Jackson Mrs. E.M., 334 Ravenhill Road
James L, 9 Eglantine Gdns.
James Mrs, 9 Eglantine Gdns.
Johnston Wm, 4 Roosevelt St.
Johnston Mrs, 4 Roosevelt St.
Johnstone Mrs. J, 6 Victoria Gardens
Jordon George, 28 Locksley Park
Jordon Mrs, 28 Locksley Park
Kell Joseph, 16 Brookvale St.
Kell Mrs, 16 Brookvale St.
Kell Arthur, 16 Brookvale St.
Kell Miss N, 16 Brookvale St.
Kelly Miss I, Waterask House, Dundrum
Keenan Miss, 55 Cooke St.
Kennedy R, 103 Cregagh Road
Kennedy Mrs. I.S., 17 Broomhill Park
Kennedy Mrs. R, 11 Stranmillis Park
Kennedy•Miss D, 11 Stranmillis Park
Kennedy Miss E, 11 Stranmillis Park
Kennedy Robert, 3 Sandhurst Rd.
Kennedy Mrs, 3 Sandhurst Rd.
Kennedy Miss M, 3 Sandhurst Rd.
Kidd Mrs. A, 47 Martinez Ave.
Kirkpatrick Mrs. J, 395 North Queen St.
Laird R.M., Gartan, Hampton Park
Laird Jas. A, Waterloo Gardens
Laird Miss M, Waterloo Gardens
Leith Mrs. E.J., 231 Cavehill Road
Lemon Mrs. H.E., 14 Ireton St.
Low T.McA., 28 St. Jude's Ave.
Low Mrs, 28 St. Jude's Ave.

Lowry Mrs. M.G., 13 Ravensdene Park
Lowry Miss M.F., 13 Ravensdene Park
McAllister Miss M, 16 Cherryvalley Gdns.
McAllister Miss N, 16 Cherryvalley Gdns.
McCafferty Wm, 15 Glanleam Drive
McCafferty Wm. H, 15 Glanleam Drive
McCafferty Mrs, 15 Glanleam Drive
McCafferty J, 7 Parkside Gdns.
McCafferty H.L., 7 Parkside Gdns.
McCafferty Miss M, 86 Mountcollyer Ave.
McCafferty Jas. R, 40 Southport Street
McCafferty Miss M.E., 40 Southport St.
McCalmont Joseph, 20 Magdala Street
McCalmont Mrs. J, 20 Magdala St.
McCandless W.H., 11 Adelaide Ave.,
   Whitehead
McCann Alexander, 17 Broomhill Park
McCrum Robt, 118 Marlborough Park
McCullough Wm, 15 Jocelyn Gardens
McCullough Mrs, 15 Jocelyn Gardens
McCutcheon Mrs. J.F.L., 23 Sailsbury
   Gardens
McCutcheon R.B., Waverley Ave., Lisburn
McDonald T, 281 Castlereagh Road
McDonald Mrs, 281 Castlereagh Road
McDonald Miss M, 281 Castlereagh Road
McDonald Miss E, 281 Castlereagh Road
McDonnell Miss G, 1 Down Villas,
   Whitehead
McFadden Mrs, 8 Adelaide Park
MacGiffin H.A., 46 Marlborough Park N.
MacGiffin Mrs, 46 Marlborough Park N.
McGuckin Mrs, 95 Eglantine Gdns.
McKee Wm, 379 Springfield Road
McKee Mrs, 379 Springfield Road
McKee W.A., Bahrian
McKelvey John, 9 Isadore Avenue
McKelvey Miss, 9 Isadore Avenue
McKelvey J.E., 3 Norwood Park
Mackenzie John, 44 Knock Eded Park
McKisack C.J., 9 Mountpleasant
McKisack A.M., 9 Mountpleasant
McKisack Miss A, 9 Mountpleasant
McKisack Miss M.K., 9 Mountpleasant
McLennan A, 26 Broughton Park
McLennan Mrs, 26 Broughton Park
McMullan Mrs. H, 31 Gainsborough Drive
McMurray T.H., 26 Cliftonville Ave.
McMurray Miss, 26 Cliftonville Ave.
McMurray Mrs. C, 5 Burmah St.
McMurray W.A., 5 Burmah St.
McMurray F, 220 Cregagh St.
McMurray Mrs. F, 220 Cregagh St.
McMurray D, 15 Broughton Gdns.
McMurray Mrs. D, 15 Broughton Gdns.
McMurray T, Massey Ave., Campbell
   College
McMurray Mrs. T, Massey Ave., Campbell
   College
McNeill, A, 54 Belmont Ave.
McNeill A.R., 3 Marlborough Park Central
McNeill Mrs. A.R., 3 Marlborough Park
   Central

McNinch Mrs. R.A., 3 Marlborough Park Central
McNinch R.J., 3 Marlborough Park Central
McNinch Thomas, 100 Donaghadee Road, Bangor
McNinch Mrs, 100 Donaghadee Road, Bangor
McRobert C.H., 80 Orby Drive
McRobert Wm, 61 Wellington Park
McRobert Mrs, 61 Wellington Park
McRobert Wm. Jun, 61 Wellington Park
McRobert Hugh, 17 Kingsland Park
McRobert Mrs. H, 17 Kingsland Park
McRoberts Mrs. M, 6 Victoria Gardens
McRoberts R.S., 44 Cliftondene Gardens
McRoberts Mrs. R.S., 44 Cliftondene Gardens
Magill Mrs. G, 6 Victoria Gardens
Major Miss, Ulai, Holywood
Martin Robert, 16 Ravenhill Park
Mawhinney Mrs. S, Galway Park, Dundonald
Meneely James, 17 Hesketh Park
Meneely Mrs, 17 Hesketh Park
Mercer Mrs. M.E., 16 Meadowbank St.
Megaw M, 1 Cregagh Park
Megaw Mrs, 1 Cregagh Park
Miller Mrs. T, 9 Silverstream Gdns.
Miller R, 19 Isadore Avenue
Miller Miss G, 19 Isadore Avenue
Miller Miss C, 19 Isadore Avenue
Miniss John B, 61 Osborne Drive
Miniss Mrs, 61 Osborne Drive
Mitchell J, 82 Ravenhill Park
Montgomery Miss K, 73 Osborne Park
Moore T, Old Rossorry, Enniskillen
Moore Mrs. E, Old Rossorry, Enniskillen
Morrow W.B.F., Richmond, Old Cavehill Road
Mulligan Miss C, Clifton House, North Queen Street
Munn S.J., Tara, Knocklofty Park
Munn Mrs, Tara, Knocklofty Park
Murphy Wm, 42 Broadway
Murphy Mrs, 42 Broadway
Murphy Robert, 42 Broadway
Nelson Miss J, Ardmore, Saintfield Road
Nelson John, 134 University St.
Nelson Mrs, 134 University St.
Nesbitt J, 32 Kensington Road
Nesbitt Mrs, 32 Kensington Road
Newel Miss J.F., Shanacloon, Upper Malone
Newman W, 34 Fitzroy Ave.
Newman Mrs, 34 Fitzroy Ave.
Newman Miss J, 34 Fitzroy Ave.
Newman Miss M, 34 Fitzroy Ave.
Newman W. Jun, Inver, Larne
Newman T, 131 Paypark Ave.
Newman Mrs, 131 Haypark Ave.
Newman Miss F, 7 Sunbury Ave.
Newman Miss M, 7 Sunbury Ave.
Orr W, Killynure, Carryduff
Orr Mrs, Killynure, Carryduff
Overend R, 3 Albany Pl., Stranraer

Parker T., 45 Camden St.
Parker Miss M.E., 45 Camden St.
Parker Miss A, 45 Camden St.
Parker Miss M, 45 Camden St.
Parker James, 45 Camden St.
Patterson Mrs, 556 Crumlin Road
Patterson M.T., 556 Crumlin Road
Patterson J.K., 55 Oakland Ave.
Radcliffe Rev. J, The Manse, Downpatrick
Rea Mrs. J, 18 Cliftonville Ave.
Robinson Mrs. S, 10 Fitzroy Ave.
Robinson S, 98 Orangefield Crescent
Robinson Mrs, 98 Orangefield Crecent
Robinson Mrs. D, 76 Canal St., Newry
Roche H.G., 60 Malone Road
Rogers Miss, 22 Derryvolgie Ave.
Rogers J.S., 16 Deramore Park
Roney Mrs. J, 52 Glandore Ave.
Russell W.H., Ulster Bank, Dublin
Russell Mrs. E, 3 Alloa St.
Russell Miss C, 3 Alloa St.
Saunders J.H., 33 Cyprus Ave.
Saunders Mrs. J.H., 33 Cyprus Ave.
Scott Alex, 7 Moira Rd., Lisburn
Scott Mrs, 7 Moira Rd., Lisburn
Scott Wm, 8 Third Avenue, Bangor
Seaye M, 1 Avoca St.
Service Mrs, 36 Lecumpher St.
Shaw Mrs. H.L., 10 Summerhill Ave.
Simonton Montague, Stockman's Lane
Smyth Mrs Malcolm Brice, 54 Malone Rd.
Smyth Miss, 16 Dunluce Ave.
Spence Jas, 28 St. Jude's Ave.
Spence Mrs, 28 St. Jude's Ave.
Spence Miss I, 43 Ligoniel Rd.
Spence Alex, 80 Church Rd., Holywood
Spence Mrs. A, 80 Church Rd., Holywood
Stepney Miss M.A., 132 Roden St.
Stewart Robt, 966 Crumlin Road
Stewart Mrs. S, 16 Woodvale Parade
Stewart Miss L, 34 Pacific Avenue
Tate W.J., 82 Ravenhill Park
Tate Mrs, 82 Ravenhill Park
Taylor Albert, 12 Cranmore Park
Taylor Mrs, 12 Cranmore Park
Walker Mrs. M, 11 Adelaide Avenue, Whitehead
Watson Mrs, 14 Ravenhill Park
Watson Miss M.E., 14 Ravenhill Park
Wilde Mrs. R.W., 20 Cadogan Park
Wilde G.H., 20 Cadogan Park
Wilkinson John, 52 North Road
Wilkinson Robert, 23 University Ave.
Wilkinson Mrs, 23 University Ave.
Williams J.R., 50 Cabin Hill Park
Williamson Miss, 1 Down Villas, Whitehead
Wilson Miss M, 13 Mount Vernon Park
Wood Mrs. W.H., 15 Shancool Park
Wood J.S., Chelmsford, Essex
Wood Miss D, 15 Shancool Park
Wood Miss M.E., 26 Brookvale Ave.
Wright Miss I, 27 Arundel St.
Young Leslie, 1 Holland Park
Young Mrs, 1 Holland Park

APPENDIX 16: ROLL OF CONSTITUENTS 1975

Alexander Mr. & Mrs, 9 Cumberland Drive
Alexander Miss H, 9 Cumberland Drive
Allison Mrs, Orlock
Arbuckle Mr. & Mrs. N.J.T., 15 Farnham
    Park Bangor
Banford Wm, 35 Beechgrove Ave.
Banford Mrs, 35 Beechgrove Ave.
Barnes Mrs, 57 King's Road
Beattie W.R., 32 Kensington Road
Beattie Mrs, 32 Kensington Road
Bell Mr. & Mrs. S, 5 Willowbank Drive
Blythe Mrs. H, 84 Newtownards Road,
    Bangor
Blythe Mr. & Mrs. B., 1 Slievecoole Park
Boas Miss M, 5 Broomhill Park
Botcher Miss B, 375 Antrim Road
Brown Mr. & Mrs. J, 6 Fourth Ave. Bangor
Campbell Mr. & Mrs. J, 3 Alloa St.
Chambers Miss E.V., 22 Cabin Hill Gdns.
Chambers J.A., Castlerocklands
Cobain Miss A, 32b Crossrea Drive
Coleman Mrs. J.R., Saintfield
Craig Mr. & Mrs. R, 32f Canberra Gardens
    Newtownards
Duddy Mr. & Mrs. R.J.T., 52 Hampton Pk.
Duffin The Misses, Bryansford Avenue,
    Newcastle
Dummigan Miss T., 23 Glenbryn Park
Dunn Miss M, Edgecumbe House
Easterbrook Mrs. M, Ascot Park
Elmes Mrs, 4 Mount Vernon Park
Ervine Miss M, 9 Downshire Road
Ervine Miss T, 9 Downshire Road
Farrell Mrs. G, 27 India Street
Fearon Mr. & Mrs. W, 18 Sunningdale
    Gardens
Fieldhouse Mrs. W, 1 Ardgreenan Mount
Fieldhouse Mr. & Mrs. M, 59 Barnetts Rd.
Fieldhouse J, 27 Radcliffe Road, London
Fletcher Mr. & Mrs. J, 53 Cotswold Ave.
Garrett J, 35 My Lady's Mile, Holywood
Gibson Miss J, Fortwilliam, Alexandra
    Gardens
Gibson Misses, 36 Old Cavehill Road
Gordon S, 6 Moyra Crescent
Graham Mrs. J, 69 Ulsterville Gdns.
Green Mrs. J, 98 Priory Park
Hall Miss M, 59 Ardenlee Ave.
Hall Mrs. M.I., 16 Ranfurly Drive
Hamill, Mrs. E, 11 Knock Rd.
Hanna J, 21 Cliftondene Pk.
Hester Mrs, 144 Whitewell Rd.
Hewitt Miss R, 67 The Mount
Hobart Mr. & Mrs. H, 10 Beechlawn Park
Hobart Miss A, 10 Beechlawn Park
Hunter Mrs. W, 28 Greenburn Park
James Dr. E, 10 Circular Road,
    Dungannon
Johnston Mrs, 4 Roosevelt St.
Johnstone Mrs. J.B., 23 Holland Park
Kell Mrs. A.E. J.P., 16 Brookvale St.

Kelly Miss I, 5 Windmill Gardens,
    Ballynahinch
Kennedy Miss D, 11 Stranmillis Park
Kennedy Mr. & Mrs. R, 3 Sandhurst Rd.
Kerr Mrs. E, 11 Knock Road
Kirk W, 9 Carnvue Gardens
Kirkpatrick J, 19 Lilliput St.
Kirkpatrick Mr. & Mrs. H, 14 Glenhurst
    Parade
Kirkwood Mr. & Mrs. A, 82 Princess Way,
    Portadown
Laird Mrs. E, 11 Hampton Park
Laird Miss D, 11 Hampton Park
Lemon Mrs. H.E., 42 Green Road
Lyle Mr. & Mrs. H.K., 210 River Road
McAllister Misses, Enler House,
    Ballybeen
McCafferty Miss M.E., Flat 27f, Abbots
    Cross
McCafferty Miss J, 144 Whitewell Road
McCafferty H.L., 23 Carwood Ave.
McCalmont Mr. & Mrs. J, 2 Ardeeghan
    Gardens
McCay Mr. & Mrs. W, 43 Maryville Park
McCombe Mr. & Mrs. D, 62 Wynchurch
    Park
McGregor Miss E, Flat 3a, Whincroft
    House
McKee Mrs. S, 23 Glenbyrn Park
McKelvey Miss I, 9 Isadore Ave.
McKeown Miss M, 59 Glandore Ave.
McLachlan P.J., 4 Parkmount, Belsize Rd.
MacLennan A, Crofton, Donaghadee
McMillan J.J., 132 Church Road,
    Newtownabbey
McMurray Mrs. I, 4 Gibson Park Avenue
McMurray C, 4 Gibson Park Avenue
McMurray Miss L, 4 Gibson Park Avenue
McMurray Mr. & Mrs. F, 28 Castleward
    Park
McMurray Mr. & Mrs. S, 10 Glen Ebor Pk.
McMurray Mr. & Mrs. D, 132 Haypark
    Avenue
McMurray Ian, 132 Haypark Avenue
McMurray Miss F, 26 Cliftonville Ave.
McNinch Capt. R.J., Belgravia Hotel
McRobert Mr. & Mrs. W, 61 Wellington
    Park
McRobert Mr. & Mrs. H, 30 Stormont Pk.
McRobert W, 30 Stormont Park
McRoberts Mr. & Mrs. R.S., 44
    Cliftondene Gardens
McWilliams Mr. & Mrs. A, 75 Northwood
    Road
Magee Mrs, 11 Ardavon Park
Mahood Mrs, 44 Cliftondene Gardens
Major The Misses, Ulai, Holywood
Malcolm The Misses, 62 Cable Road,
    Whitehead
Mann Mrs. J, 26 Millfield, Ballymena
Mateer Mrs. G, 27 Woodvale Rd.

154

Mee Mrs, 11 Holland Park
Mee Miss A, 11 Holland Park
Megaw Mrs, 1 Cregagh Park
Meneely Mrs. V, 77 Abbey Park
Meneely Miss R, 77 Abbey Park
Miniss J.B., Belgravia Hotel
Montgomery Miss K, 14 Adelaide Park
Montgomery Mr. & Mrs. T, 122b Upper
  Lisburn Road
Moore Mr. & Mrs. A, 100 Meenan St.
Moore Mr. & Mrs. T, 5 Cairnburn Ave.
Morrow J.H.G., 89 Merville Garden
  Village
Munn Mrs. D.L., 13 Greenwood Park
Munn Miss E.B., 13 Greenwood Park
Murphy Mrs. E.H., 18a Dakota Avenue,
  Newtownards
Murphy Mr. & Mrs. Ivan, 27 Portaferry
  Road, Newtownards
Murphy Mr. & Mrs. W, 410 Shore Road
Nelson Mrs. E, 39 Saintfield Road
Nesbitt Miss M, 6 Glantane St.
Newell Miss E, 24 Duffield Park
Newman The Misses, 35a Black's Road
Newman Mr. & Mrs. T, 39 Ravenhill Park
Newman Miss F, 7 Sunbury Ave.
Newman Miss M, 7 Sunbury Ave.
Newman Miss A, 57 King's Road
Parker Miss M.E., 45 Camden St.
Parker J, 45 Camden St.
Parker Miss M, 45 Camden St.
Patterson Mrs. A, 57 Edinburgh St.
Porter Mr. & Mrs. D, 20 East Mount,
  Newtownards
Pyper Mrs. M.A., 4 Fernmore Ave., Bangor
Radcliffe Rev. J, The Manse, Downpatrick
Rea Mrs. R, 24 Duncoole Park
Reid F.A., 32b Windsor Park

Robinson Mr. & Mrs. S, 40 Cyprus Gdns.
Robinson W, 1 Sandhurst Road
Robinson Mr. & Mrs. J, 51 Knockbracken
  Park
Robinson G, 51 Knockbracken Park
Robinson A, 51 Knockbracken Park
Russell Mrs. M, 3 Sandhurst Road
Saunders Mrs. D.M., 7 Sunbury Ave.
Seaye Mrs. M, 1 Onslow Park
Sharpe R, 114 Orangefield Crecent
Simpson Miss M, 4 Knock Road
Smyth F.D., 23 Broughton Gdns.
Stewart Mrs. S, 16 Woodvale Pde.
Stewart J, 16 Woodvale Pde.
Stewart R, 966 Crumlin Rd.
Thompson Mr. & Mrs. R, 9 East Mount St.,
  Newtownards
Thompkins Mrs. N.E., 50 Ashley Ave.
Trueick Mr. & Mrs. R, 170 Donaghadee
  Road, Bangor
Wallace Mr. & Mrs. R, 11 Knock Road
Watters Mrs. L, 3b Cappagh Gdns.
Weaver Miss B, Wandsworth Parade
Webb Mr. & Mrs. J.A., 36 Lynne Road,
  Bangor
Williams J.R., 29 Kensington Road
Wilson Mr. & Mrs. J, 15 Windsor Gardens
Wilson Miss M, 4 Mount Vernon Walk
Wood Miss D, Ealing, London
Wood J.S., 144 Vicarage Rd., Chelmsford
Wood Miss M.E., Fortwilliam, Alexander
  Gardens
Wood Capt. W.H., 144 Vicarage Road,
  Chelmsford
Wright Mr. & Mrs. N, 44 James St.
Young Mr. & Mrs. L, Lissue House,
  Lisburn

Sconce now in session room
Photo: Philip McConnell

INDEX

Abjuration, Oath of	24, 126	Lease of site	29
Academical Institution	104	Leslie, Bishop of Down	10
Air Raids	47	Leslie, Bishop of Raphoe	19
Andrews, Thomas	117	Lynn, W. H.	34
Baird, Rev. J.	11	Manson, David	103
Belfast Academy	104	Melville, Andrew	5
Blair, Rev. Robert	10	Milton, John	8, 125
Blood, T.	20	Monk, General	13, 19
Bomb Damage	42	Monro, General	11
Bramhall, John	10, 19	Montgomery, Rev. Dr. H.	25
Breda, Declaration of	8	Mountpottinger Church	113
Broadcast Services	91	Mulholland, Roger	31
Bruce, Rev. Dr. Wm.	121, 128	McBride, Rev. J.	24, 126
Calvin, J.	4	McLachlan, Rev. Dr. H. J.	117, 123
Central Hall	44	McTier, S.	118
Chamberlain, Neville	123	Necessary Representation	125
Charles I	7	Organ Chamber	35
Charles II	8	Ormond, Duke of	20
Chichester, Sir A.	11	Pike, Rev. J. K.	62
Church of Rome	2	Poor School	103
Commonwealth	8	Porter, Rev. J. Scott	128
Communion Services	89	Portico	33
Cooke, Rev. Dr. H.	25, 105	Presbytery of Antrim	25
Coote, Sir C.	13	Protestant Reformation	4
Crombie, Rev. Dr. J.	32, 104, 127	Regium Donum	22
Cromwell, Henry	17	Remonstrant Synod	25
Cromwell, Oliver	8	Riddel Memorial School	111
Drennen, Dr. Wm.	52, 105, 119	Rules & Regulations	74
Echlin, Bishop	10	Sacramental Test	23
Ecumenism	123	Scots Army in Ulster	11
Ede, Rt. Hon. J. C.	123	Seating capacity of church	32
Education, Non-sectarian	106	Second congregation	24
Elizabeth I	4	Shaw, Rev. A.	13
Engagement	16	Sinclair, T.	118
Fennell	46	Solemn League & Covenant	6
Fleetwood	16	Stained glass windows	41
Fountain Street School	106	Taylor, Bishop Jeremy	19
Gallery	32	Telephone Service	116
Gibson & Taylor	49	Titanic	117
Gordon, Rev. Alex	129	Theaker, Thos.	12
Grindal	5	Third Congregation	24
Haliday, Rev. S.	127	United Irishmen	121
Haliday, Dr.	52, 119	Unitarianism	132
Hampton Court Conference	6	Venables, Col.	14
Harland, Sir E. J.	46	Volunteers	118
Henry VIII	4	War Memorials	42, 51
Hiorne	32	Walmsley, Rev. D.	65
Hollins, Alfred	35	Wentworth	10
Isherwood & Ellis	43	Westminster Confession of Faith	7, 24
James I	6	Whitgift, John	5
James II	21	William III	21
Keyes, Rev. Wm.	18, 126	Wilde, Rev. Dr. R. W.	47, 130
Kirk, Andrew	53	Young & Mackenzie	47
Knox, John	5	York Street Church	47
Lead Box	48		